IASGACH AN ALBA

FISHING SCOTLAND

Argyll
the Isles
Loch Lomond
Stirling & Trossachs

Cover design and illustrations by Robin Kyle

SCOTLAND

R. Kyle 95

By the same author:
Game Fishing Guide to Inverness-shire 1967
Game Fishing Guide to Argyll-shire 1967
Game Fishing Guide to Shetland 1968
Game Fishing Guide to Orkney 1968
Game Fishing Guide to the Outer Hebrides 1969
Game Fishing Guide to Sutherland & Caithness 1969
Game Fishing Guide Inverness-shire, Isle of Skye & Moray & Nairn 1995
Game Fishing Guide Inverness-shire, Isle of Skye & Moray & Nairn 1996
Game Fishing Guide Ross/Cromarty - Sutherland/Caithness 1996
Game fishing guide Argyll & Islands & Loch Lomond 1996
Game Fishing guide Inverness-shire - Isle of Skye - Moray & Nairn 1997
Game Fishing Guide Ross & Cromarty - Sutherland & Caithness 1997
Game Fishing Guide Argyll Isles Loch Lomond Stirling Trossach's 1997
Game Fishing guide Inverness-shire - Isle of Skye - Moray & Nairn 1998
Game Fishing Guide Ross & Cromarty - Sutherland & Caithness 1998
Game Fishing Guide Argyll Isles Loch Lomond Stirling Trossach's 1998
Game Fishing guide Inverness-shire - Isle of Skye - Moray & Nairn 1999
Game Fishing Guide Ross & Cromarty - Sutherland & Caithness 1999

A record of this book is available from the British Library
ISBN: 1 900417 10 3
Published by Fishing Scotland
Printed by NEVISPRINT - FORT WILLIAM
Illustrations and cover art by:
Robin Kyle 10 Seafield Gardens Fort William PH33 6RJ

While every effort is made to ensure information and charges detailed are
current, no responsibility is accepted for change, alteration, cancellation
or non availability of fishing, permit or services implied or considered in
this book.

FISHING SCOTLAND Roy Bridge Inverness-shire PH31 4AG
Tel/Fax: (01397) 712 812
www.Fishing-Scotland.co.uk
email: info@fishing-scotland.co.uk

Preface

My first fishing guide, in 1966, was written because I was bothered by the amount of good fishing time I used up just hunting out new waters in the Highlands. I know the Highlands very well, so what must it be like for visitors! Your fishing time is just as precious, so I hope the information in this wee book will assist in providing more fishing time and add some little to the pleasure.

This 1999 edition covers Argyll, the Isles, Loch Lomond, Stirling & Trossachs and the wonderful fishing that area has to offer.

Not all waters where a good day's sport is to be had are listed here. Some waters may be fished simply by making a mannerly request to the owner or keeper. These waters I leave to be found by initiative.

You will find that I have recorded fair assessments and expectations with consideration of the vagaries of angling.

One subject I would open here is the misconception that the lochs and river of this great land of ours can continue to provide fish, the wee troot no less, together with salmon and sea trout without research prepared planning and good management. There are too many fishers now for nature to balance the taking without assistance in conservation.

To sustain and continue to provide sport fishing has a price, with modest cost to the angler. Protection orders are here to stay. With the letter of their intention followed, as most experianced anglers do, good fishing will be sustained if not improved, for all. The newly formed Trusts of the west coast and their intended cooperative resource research is a great step forward. Genuine and knowledgable participation of associations and clubs is a priority if these programs are to succeed. Casual and expert alike must fish within knowledgable considered paramiters, be conservation minded and leave the country and waterside at least as is for those who follow.

Thanks you all, fishers, ghillies, keepers, tackle merchants, hoteliers, club officials and staff of every Tourist Information Centre in the region who shared thoughts and expressed experience and considerations of this wonderful country, its fauna, flora and all things fishing.

Aye,

James Coutts

January 1999
Roy Bridge
Inverness-shire PH31 4AG

SAFETY CONSIDERATIONS

Fishing like other water oriented recreations or pastimes requires continual awareness of the hazards of being in, on or close to that environment. The consequences of an error of judgement, accident or the thoughtlessness of others **may well result in drowning.**

Whether you can swim or not, a properly fitting life jacket or buoyancy aid should be worn on your person while in any small boat or close to water.

Alcohol contributes to more boating accidents than all other causes.

Standing up or moving about within a boat is the major cause of man overboard and capsize accidents.

Overloading is a common cause of accidents.

COLD CAN KILL - IF IN DOUBT! DO NOT GO OUT

THE LAW WHILE FISHING IN SCOTLAND

The following is intended to ensure the reader will be aware of likely instances of law infringement or where confrontation may occur.

It is an offence for any person to fish for or take salmon or sea trout without written permission.

It is prohibited throughout Scotland to fish for or take salmon or sea trout on a Sunday.

A fishing permit covers one rod only, unless otherwise specified.

Fishing rods must be hand held. Rod/s set up on river bank or loch shores are set lines and are illegal in Scotland.

The open season to fish for brown trout is from 15th March through 6th October. Frequently, this period is lawfully curtailed.

A **Protection Order** in effect, is the instrument of protection of an area of water under management to improve viable fishing. It is an offence to fish a protected water without a current permit on your person. The permit charge on such waters is used directly to effect and improve and possibly develop that water **for the rod and line angler.**

Private property access is NOT open to any person who does not have the permission of the owner/s.

A mannerly request or inquiry may well avoid a confrontation.

If in any doubt! Check locally - before fishing

LEARN FLY FISHING

Learn to cast a fly for wild brown trout and rainbow trout at select Highland lochs, in the heart of Lochaber.

The habitat of eagle, otter and red deer, each loch is just a stroll from easy road access, in rugged Highland grandeur.

Totally inclusive day and evening excursions – Hotel pick-up by arrangement
Individual & small group instruction – families & young people welcome corporate groups
Excursions of three or more days by arrangement

Who will catch the first salmon of the year 2000?
Millennium Atlantic Salmon "Learn to Fish' all inclusive
Short break private excursions from 15th January 2000

PRE - RESERVATION ESSENTIAL
FISHING SCOTLAND
ROY BRIDGE INVERNESS-SHIRE PH31 4AG
TEL/FAX (01397) 712 812
www.fishing-scotland.co.uk
email: info@fishing-scotland.co.uk

CONTENTS

PART ONE
OBAN - NORTH LORN - GLEN COE

In a wonderful scenic position overlooking the Firth of Lorn the harbour town of Oban has still the atmosphere of a small west coast village though it is one of the main visitor destinations of Argyll. **The Tourist Information Centre Tel: (01631) 563 122** is strategically placed in Argyll Square and bursting with literature and all the knowledgeable information and advice the visitor expects. The angler who is gregarious by nature and prefers town accommodation will find, above the sheltered harbour, all manner of hostelries, hotels, guest houses, B & B in profusion and plenty of caravan and camping parks near by. Loch, river, and burn fishing abound in the surrounding hills and glens with excellent sea fishing along the coast line or from boats rented or chartered at the harbour. **The Oban and Lorn Angling Club** manages 27 lochs, some with boats, fine fishing indeed at very modest charges. **Mackays Loch,** stocked with rainbow trout and with a good head of native Brown Trout is only a five minute drive from Main street. Permits for **Mackays Loch** are available only at **Anglers Corner, 2 John Street,** just off Main Street. They also issue permits for the local Association waters as well as an endless selection of all manner of fresh and sea fishing tackle in a friendly west Highland manner. David Graham Tackle and Cycles on Combie Street just off Argyll Square also issue association permits and all the right fishing tackle for local conditions.

The **Caledonian MacBrayne** Company run regular ferry services to the following islands: Coll and Tiree (5 hr); Castlebay (5 1/4 hr); Lochboisdale (6 hr); Colonsay (2 1/2 hr); Craignure (40min) Day cruises to Kerrera, Lismore, Mull and Iona provide wonderful views of the rugged mainland mountains and forests. Forest Enterprise have provided some excellent bike trails and walking routes in this area with super detail maps and guides available free from local Forest Enterprise offices. Golf, horse trekking, tennis, Sail and motor boat hire, Diving and all such good stuff is readily available locally.

North of Oban is an expanse of mountain and glen with ancient castles, monuments, buildings and sites of great historic significance. Visit the 11th century Priory at Ardchattan where the last Gaelic speaking parliament was held. Great beauty and majesty surrounds one on the journey north skirting the sea Lochs Creran, Linnhe and then Leven the mountains of Lochaber rising from the northern shore. The three sisters of Glen Coe still the very same immovable mountains and streams that witnessed the birth of Highland culture. South through Glen Coe by way of the A82 is a pleasure of scenic value regardless of the weather. This great glen and the surrounding country is the property of the National Trust for Scotland who have a very special visitor centre on the banks of the River Coe just a mile into the glen and should not be missed. The new road dating from 1935, takes lower levels than the previous stage route which followed a drove road visible at various stages of the assent to the Muir of Rannoch bordered to the north by the Mamore Mountains while the Mountains of north Lorn tower above the road as it climbs again, over Black Mount to sweep down with spectacular views of Loch Tulla to Bridge of Orchy Hotel on the West Highland Way. Just passed the hotel take the B8074 through Glen Orchy rather than the A82, it hugs the bank of the river and is a splendid mostly treed glen with quiet ambiance and joins the A85 to Oban just east of Dalmally.

OBAN and LORN ANGLING CLUB

The club, formed in 1972 has the objectives of improving and providing fishing in the Lorn district of Argyll for both visiting and local anglers.. Some of the hill lochs are in quite remote areas and require prior planning with consideration of the likelihood of snow until the end of May and heavy frost possible from the beginning of August. Wind and waterproof clothing and stout footwear are essential at all times of the season, as is extra food, a map, compass, torch and whistle. Midge repellent and or a net will add to comfort as will extra dry clothing both in your bag and in the car. If you must go it alone, ensure someone responsible knows where you are heading, your route and intended return time. Anglers are asked to record returns and to return to the water any fish taken with clipped adipose fin. Spinning and Bubble float fly are permitted only on the Oude Reservoir. Only one rod permitted each permit. Set lines are illegal. There are boats on many lochs, inquire at the tackle shop when you collect your permit. Bailiffs and members monitor all waters, permits must be purchased before fishing.

1999 Permit Outlets and Charges

The Angler Corner 2 John Street Oban PA34 5NS (01631) 566 374;
D. Graham & Son 9-15 Combie Street Oban PA34 4HN (01631) 562 069;
Post Office, Kilmelford; Cuilfail Hotel, Kilmelford; Kilchrenan Inn;
Ledaig Motors, Benderloch.

**Visitor day permits: £10.00 - Three to seven days £25.00 -
Day Boat permit £8.00**
Annual Member £20 plus £10 joining fee
Senior citizen £8 plus £5.00 joining fee
**Reintroduced in 1999 will be the Associate Annual Ticket for those
who live outside the Oban Lorn area: Annual Associate £20.00**

NO FLOAT TUBES PERMITTED

Salmon and Sea Trout   Season: 11 February - 15 October
Brown Trout   Season: 15 March - 6 October

The following indicates typical quality and location to expect. Locally
favoured for sea trout and salmon are **ABU Toby, Bridun Hunter and
Mepps.** Flies **Butcher, Peter Ross, Watson's Fancy, Grouse and
Claret, and Invicta in size 10 to 14** for brownies with any **teal winged,
Butcher or Zulu in 8 to 10** preferred for sea trout and salmon.

LOCH NELL   Brown Trout, Sea Trout and Salmon.

Due to reorganisation and conservation considerations by the proprietors the
Angling Association it would appear will not have fishing on Loch Nell in
1999.

SOIR LOCHS (SHEER LOCHS)

Just full of wee troot what will please the beginner to fly fishing or an ideal
place to introduce a non fisher to the sport. The remote glen situation and the
prolific bird life will ease away any stress and relieve tension like magic. Pro-
ceed as for Loch Nell to the T junction, turn right, at 4 miles, park in the quarry
past the Kilchrenan footpath sign, walk the path for 15 minutes and turn left
onto the Hydro road to the loch. Fishes best in April and May with wee flies of
the 12 to 14 size, try Dark Mackerel and Black Pennel. Weed from June on can
be a problem.

LOCH A'BHARRAIN (Ah Varr-ane)

From the Sior Loch follow the burn due north to this wee peaty watered loch with wee troot. A nice walk, a fine situation of peace and
quiet where few anglers tread.

OUDE Reservoir (Ood)

Go south on the A816 for 14 miles, the reservoir is on the right hand side of the road. Bank fishing can sometimes be a problem due to fluctuating water levels, be aware of soft wet peat. There is a club boat on this water on occasions which makes for easy fishing for the free rising trout of maybe three to the pound.

LOCH AN LOSGAINN MOR (an Lus-gan mor)

Take the Loch Avich road by the post office in Kilmelford off the A816 to the top of the first hill, the loch is that on the right side of the road. The west end can be very good as is the bay to the west of the narrows. Stocked every year, trout are of 3/4lb on average. There is usually a boat on this water. Very easy of access and a good place for the family picnic not to mention that there is a string of lochs within walking distance if a change of scenery takes your fancy.

LOCH AN LOSGAINN BEAG (an lus-gan Beag)

Follow the tractor track on the other side of the road from the north west corner of Loch an Losgainn Mor, go due north over the hill and the wee loch is below. One of those mystic wee places with huge trout that are very difficult to catch! Could be that it would fish well in the evening as dusk approaches! Especially if you can catch a fly hatch and pull the wool over these fish eyes with a wee dry badger or a heather moth if it happens to be August?

BIG FEINN LOCH (Fee-an)

As for Loch an Losgainn Beag but turn right at the top of the hill, skirt passed Loch a'Mhinn and then Loch na Curraig on your right. Continue down through Glean Mor passed a ruined sheiling, cross the glen and climb the other side to the left of where the burn runs down, up to your left is a rocky escarpment, would you believe the loch lies on the top. Its a good hour walk from the road but is not a severe climb. Is it worth it! The loch is reputed to hold very large difficult to catch trout, from shore or the boat located here. The writers choice would be late April, May or June and only if there was a good breeze to create wave conditions for size 8 or 10 Invicta, Blue charm, and Black Spiders.

WEE FEINN LOCH

50 meters to the west of Big Feinn with a connecting burn this much smaller loch produces native trout up to 2lb with great regularity. Like the others in this group it is easy bank fishing and one that you may fish

for just an hour or so on a day where you might cast on six or seven, wondering from loch to loch enjoying the wonderful aspect of no schedule or time limit to cast or not to cast.

LOCH A'CHAORAINN (Ah Hoo-ran)

This is one of a group of 8 lochs to the west of those already described in the hills between Kilmelford and Loch Avich. There will be a boat here for 1999. The size, nature and proximity to each other allow perhaps four or five to be fished in an early start day. Drive for close to 1/ 3 a mile past Loch an Losgainn Mor, park at the forestry road entrance on the left before the bridge. Walk the forestry road to the parking area and carry on due north over flat marsh into the glen. At the far side where the burn comes down a gorge, climb the gorge keeping the burn to your left, follow the path till you cross the burn, cross the stile on the deer fence, continue on north parallel to the fence on the right until you reach the loch. Pretty difficult terrain which takes about 45 minutes without rushing. A stocked loch (1 to 2lb brownies), could be creating close to a heart attack if they connect before you cool down after the walk in. There is a boat usually located here. Some say this is a dour loch, however well presented flies as close to those you see hatching or terrestrials alighting should provide some action.

Follow the burn flowing out of the north corner of the loch for 150 meters to **LOCH A' CHREACHAIN (Ah Creech-an)** A lot of small fish in this loch are supplemented by 1 to 2lb stock and these fighting fit troot are regular takers that seem to come on with the presentation of bigger flies of the lure type. Try a double or treble worm fly size 8. There will not be a boat here in 1999.

Follow the burn which runs into the first bay on the right, cross the deer fence by the stile, to **LOCH DUBH-BHEAG (Doo-beg)** Steep heather banking should be traversed with caution in this difficult to wade lochan which has been stocked with brownies additional to the natives. The trout are good free risers and can be expected to weight in at up to 1lb.

Follow the burn flowing into the bay on the east side for 200mt climb slope to the left, to: **LOCHAN CRUACH MAOLACH (Croo-ach Moo-lachy)** Stocked trout here reach at least 2lb and are said to be some of the best conditioned trout in the area.

LOCH AVICH

The association leases a section of the west bank fishing here which extends to the first little headland on the north shore round the west end and along the south shore to just past the island on the opposite shore. For fishing information refer to Loch Avich in the Loch Awe section.

LOCH NANT

This large loch is situated in the hills to the west of Glen Nant through which the B845 climbs from Taynuilt to Kilchrenan. A gate Hydro road leads up to the loch, however, anglers are permitted only on foot, it is a two mile walk. A loch of fluctuating levels it fishes best when the water is at a lower level. Due to the elevation Nant does not come on until mid May but with good conditions produces heavy trout continuing through June and July then September again sees fine activity. Some caution is required due to the infirm peat hags and soft silt especially at low water levels.

LOCH SCAMADALE

Salmon and Sea Trout   **Season June - 15 October**

Just beyond the ninth milestone on Loch Feachan side on the A816 Oban to Lochgilphead road, at the brow of a wee hill a signpost indicates **Loch Scamadale** to the left. A good single track road hugs the River Euchar all the way to emerge in a lost world with a beautiful loch and grand Highland mountains.

The salmon follow the steep runs of the River Euchar to enter the loch at its west end, always supposing there is some water to encourage them make the dash. Close to 2 miles long the Loch fishing is equally good from bank or boat with deep water shelving from just a few feet from the shore line at most places. It is on this shelf that the migratory fish lie, so that, being so near the shore it is by stealth and quiet that the fisher is likely to approach without disturbing fish. Fish enter the loch from July or August. Early on, the west end of the loch is tops but as the fish prepare to enter the burns and streams of the east end that is where they congregate. Flies should be of **8 to 10** unless there is no wind with Watson's Fancy, Dunkeld, Cinnamon and Gold, and Coachman found to be very satisfactory. Spinning is permitted, however Sunday fishing is not. **Bank fishing costs £3 per rod** with a maximum of 8 available, a **boat for up to 2 rods is £12** all excellent value. Permits and information on fishing and farmhouse accommodation including self-catering should be directed to: **Mrs McCorkindale Snr, "Glenann" Scamadale, Argyll PA34 4UU (01852) 316 282**

RIVER EUCHAR - TOP BEAT

There are three beat on this fine wee stream where day permits can be available. Each beat has holding pools which fish best in falling water after a spate. Sea trout and salmon are expected from mid June with numbers increasing through July till close of season on 15 October. Access from the road is excellent with the added advantage of being a safe and very pleasant place for family picnics.

From the loch downstream for a distance of just over 1/2 a mile three rods are permitted at the modest charge of £3. There are three nice pools which depend on outflow from the loch and have the bonus of the loch to fish if conditions should deteriorate. Fly and Spinning is permitted. **Permits from Mrs McCorkindale at the loch side.**

LAGGAN BEG BEAT

The middle beat of the river is about 3/4 of a mile long with holding pools similar to the higher beat and is available only on Tuesday, Wednesday and Thursday. Access is again very good with peace and quiet assured . Fly and spinning allowed. Permits and details of fishing and holiday bungalows from: Mrs. Eve Mellor, Barndromin farm, Knipoch, Argyll (01852) 316 273

LAGGAN MORE BEAT

This lower stretch of the river is almost a mile long extending from the lower limit of the Laggan Beg beat to the road bridge and is on occasions available. A fly only water, in condition includes some really nice casts. From the road bridge to the estuary is private water, Details from: Andrew Sandilands, Lagganmore, Argyll (01852) 316 205

MACKAYS LOCH - FLY ONLY

Rainbow and Brown Trout   Season open all year for Rainbow
Regularly stocked as required with rainbow trout and with a good head of native Brown Trout this popular loch is only ten minutes by car from Oban town centre in a quiet glen with Natural surroundings including mature hardwood and shrubs which do not in anyway curtail access and casting since efficient platforms are installed at strategic

locations. A half day costs £10 and a full day £16. Boats for up to 2 rods are available at just £5 extra on the bank permit charge, which should be booked in advance particularly at the weekends and throughout the summer months when this well shaded location gets lots of attention from the local fly fishing fraternity. Ample car parking at the lochside makes for convenience. **Permits and inquiries to: Anglers Corner, 2 St John St. Oban (01631) 566 374 or Ivan Nicolson, Barranrioch, Glencruitten, Oban PA34 4QI (01631) 770223.**

HOSPITAL (GLEN COE) LOCHAN - Rainbow trout.

Forest Enterprise are to be congratulated on the fine job they have done here. Stocked with rainbow trout of around the 3/4lb mark, provided with floating casting platforms, access for wheelchair fishing from the bank or a special boat. Bank fishing day permits are £5 each with a 4 fish limit. Junior permits are £2.50. Boat permits for two rods are £15 for one session or £20 for two sessions. 09:00 till 13:00. 13.00 till 17:15 & 17:15 till 21:30. The loch is situated on hospital hill and permits are issued at Scorry Breac Guest House Tel: (01855) 811 354 (first on the left up the hospital drive) and at Glencoe Camp Shop (01855) 811 397.

LOCH DUBH RESERVOIR

A forestry loch reached by a 1km walk on a green route from Sutherland Grove just 1km north of Barcaldine on the A828. Access is easy with just mild walking to this wee loch inhabited by Rainbow and lots of wee Brown trout. **Permits are £3 from Mrs Lyon, Appin View, Barcaldine or Anglers Corner, 2 John St, Oban (01631) 566 374**

LOCH GLEAN A BHEARRAIDH

A wild brown trout loch just south of Oban a couple of miles. Great for a few hours fishing time with minimal travel time from Oban. At £3.00 a day it's a steal for three to the pound brownies. Permits from **Anglers Corner, 2 John St. Oban. Tel: (01631) 566 374**

LOCH TROUICHATAN & RIVER COE - NATIONAL TRUST

Due to bank and pool reconstruction and other work in this area there will be no fishing permits available for these Nation Trust of Scotland waters for the 1999 fishing season.

8

LOCH BA AND LOCHANS NA STAINGE AND H-ACHLAISE

Situated north of Black Mount just before the road climbs that mountain on the very edge of Glen Coe to drop down passed Loch Tulla to Bridge of Orchy. On the western edge of the great Muir of Rannoch back-dropped by a string of mountains all over 3000 ft lies a string of lochs which hold innumerable wee fish affectionately known as Tammy Troot. These lochs are easy found, for the main A82 passes between them and you are very likely to stop just to take a photograph, such is the grandeur of the scene in any kind of weather. Grandest of all in "Lightening, thunder and in rain" to quote the three witches of Macbeth who lived just north of this place. Over the years this water was much abused by some who came armed with three and more rods. These methods are all illegal, One fisher, one rod, no set lines (you must hold the rod) and so the wee troot are recovering somewhat and able to give a little sport and provide the odd breakfast for the fly fisher of initiative. Bank fishing only, no boat launching permitted, The charge! That you leave this gem of wild country as you found it. "It's magic" enjoy.

Fly Fishing

Mackays Loch is fully stocked with rainbow trout and has
a good natural stock of native brown trout. The loch is available
for fly fishing only, either from the shore, or casting platforms.
Boats are also available for hire.

The loch is situated ten minutes by car from Oban town centre. It is
easily accessible from the road and ample off road parking is provided.
Part or full day permits. Part day is any 6 hours (3 fish),
full day (5 fish) 9am till dusk.

Permits & inquiries
Anglers Corner, 2 John Street, Oban (01631) 566 374
or
Ivan Nicholson, Barranriock Farm, Glencruitten, Oban PA34 4QI (01631) 770 223
OPEN ALL YEAR

PART TWO

LOCH AWE and TRIBUTARIES

Lying almost northeast to southwest in central Argyll this 23 mile long is equally diverse in fish content as is the nature of the loch and the surrounding countryside. Its reputation, with that of the many rivers and burns that feed it and the innumerable hill lochs nearby, have since ancient times drawn the ardent fisher to the area. With the advent of rainbow trout farming cages in the loch, the inevitable escapees have added a new dimension to the specie list with no apparent detrimental side effects apart to the self esteem of the 2lb Rainbow who in affray finds it difficult to match the spunk of the 3/4lb Wild Brown Trout. Bank fishing is very popular and again, the right place with the right knowledge produces fine catches by fly, spinning and bait fishing. Traditional boat fishing takes some beating and fortunately excellent boats are available at two locations. The Lochs reputation for its huge Ferox is legendary. Double figure fish are commonplace to the new generation of Ferox fishers. The River Avich and Loch Avich are popular alternatives to the big loch and have been producing fine returns consistently for many years. Recent seasons have reflected good returns on Ederline hill lochs and the forestry Lochs Cam, Dalach, Dubh and a'Bruic which feed the River Liever. It is now mid May before salmon are expected to be resident throughout the system. The Orchy system continued with good results 97 and 98. **Loch Awe Stores** in the village of that name on the A85 has fishing tackle and permits for the rivers Orchy and Awe.

The loch shores are encircled by roads of varying classification which, though of very good quality, are narrow and require close attention when walking, driving or cycling. There are two nice forestry picnic places on the B840 at Ardray and a mile further on at Latham's Grove in the Eredine forest. Though few actual car parks there is ample parking around the loch if you are observant, but take care not to block entrances. Nearing the top end of the loch, at the narrow's is Ardbrecknish and **Donald Wilson's Loch Awe Boats** location which is adjacent to Ardbrecknish House, a self catering establishment which also offers bar and meals services.

Just east of Taynuilt on the A85 is **Inverawe Angling Centre** with its

Fly Only Rainbow Lochs, River Awe Fishing, shop and Smokery. It's a very rural establishment with high quality fishing and instruction.

The B845, off the A85 a mile east of Taynuilt village climbs with spectacular hill, forest then loch views with numerous forestry parking and picnic places the length of the north shore. Steep mountains side the loch as the road winds and climbs down through Inverinan to Dalavich village. **Norman Clark** runs **Lochaweside Marine** and has a fleet of boats on The Big Loch, (Loch Awe) at Davalich which is not far from **The Ford Hotel** at the south end of **Loch Awe**. Additionally Norman has boats on **Loch Avich** a smaller loch with great reputation above the village. The Forestry Commision Holiday Cabin park is on the loch shore at Davalich and must be one of the most scenic in the country with fishing on the front doorstep and numerous forest and hill walks out the back door. Not least **Lochaweside Marine** is right next door.

West Highland Estates Office are a good contact for salmon and trout fishing and indeed stalking and rough shooting and estate self catering cottages in this area. **Tel: (oban) 01631 563 617 (Fort William) 01397 702 433**

LOCH AWE IMPROVEMENT ASSOCIATION
PROTECTION ORDER 1992 NUMBER 771 (S.79)

Freshwater fishing without legal right or written permission is prohibited in Loch Awe, Loch Avich and the River Avich.

In the short time the association has operated there has been a marked improvement in the behaviour of fishing legally, considerate parking and refuse disposal. Please abide by the rules of the association, be a friend of the loch, enjoy and return soon. If you are not going to eat your catch! Please return it in good condition to the water. Day/weekly permits are issued at **Loch Awe Stores**, tackle stores, hotels and general stores throughout the local and Greater Glasgow area. Applications for season ticket/annual membership and inquiries should be directed to:

T C MacNair Secretary/Treasurer
Loch Awe Improvement Association
Boswell House - Argyll Square
Oban - Argyll PA34 4BD
Tel: (01631) 562 215 Fax: 565 490

1999 SEASON AND CHARGES
SUNDAY FISHING PERMITTED

Salmon and Sea Trout fishing is NOT covered by L.A.I.A. Permit
Permits: Season £36 - Weekly £12 - 3 Day £6 - 1 Day Permit £3
50% reduction on Senior Citizens, juvenile and disabled permits
Warden/Bailiff assistance call: Brian Stewart (01866) 833 270

Close season (except pike) 7 October - 14 March inclusive
Pike fishing is permitted throughout the year, including Sundays, has a
special permit and restrictions available from the secretary.

LOCH AWE

There have been gradual changes over a number of seasons on this BIG
loch. One time March, April May and September were the top months.
However June July and August are now providing equally good sport.
1998 opening day provided large catches of both Wild Brown Trout and
rainbow. Kilchrenan A.C. had ten rods fishing that day and brought 90
rainbow and 50 browns to the net. Shore fishing fared just as good and
the first Big fish of the season went to Sandy Corbett on the 16 March, a
super Wild Brown Trout of 13lb. 2oz. A very dry spell in May and June
slowed thing a mite and July turned into a great month for brown trout
in finest condition. Ferox specialist had a good season with the top fish
of 20lb. being netted and returned by Jack MacIntosh.

Popular flies are traditional loch patterns of Grouse and Claret, Peter
Ross, Woodcock and Yellow, Coachman in size 10 or 12 and as the summer progresses smaller dark flies get most attention. Trolling lures favoured are **Abu Toby and Brydun (made in Scotland) spoons.** There
are 20 fishing boats and other craft for hire at **Loch Awe Boats (01866)
833 256,** Ardbrecknish. This National Competition venue covers the north
end and island drifts. Salmon permits are also available here. On the
south west shore Dalavich where the River Avich drops down from Loch
Avich is excellent trout water. **Lochaweside Marine, Norman Clark
Esq,. (01866) 844 209** has boats here and **Loch Avich** at £27 a day
including motor and fuel or £15 without. Norman rents canoes, issues
permits, rents tackle and is most knowledgable of the whole loch which
he tells me continues to produce numerous huge pike as well as rainbow escapees up to 20lb. At the south end of the loch the **Ford Hotel** has
boats, issues permits, offers full service accommodation - has a great
public bar and serves casual meals till very late.

LOCH AVICH - RIVER AVICH

A good road from Dalavich on Loch Awe to Kilmelford on the A816 passes the loch side and gives easy access to park close to the boats or for bank fishing. Being at a higher level than the Awe it takes a wee bit longer to come into condition. A real beauty of a brownie, which weighed in at 71/2lb was landed in 97. The brownies are marginally lighter in average than the Awe troot, are just as cantankerous though and fairly wallop the fly when the urge is there, especially if you fish the favoured (12 or 14) black flies like Black Spider, Pennel, Blae and Black. There is a Mayfly hatch usually in June when Yellow, Olive and Green flies bring home the breakfast. The shallow indented bays fish well with the long one on the north shore being my own favourite when a westerly drifts the boat nicely from the island eastward. If it's honkin' and a good wave is breaking size up to 8s and try Soldier Palmer, Invicta and from late July a **real hairy Heather Moth** will bring the big fellows crashing through the waves. Boats are at a pre-mium here from May on so contact **Lochaweside Marine (01866) 844 209)** early. The river is a nice tumbling stream of little less than 1 1/2 miles. The rocky nature and tree line to the banking make for difficult fishing most of the way, certainly for the fly fisher. Worm is the local bait, and with the exception of the pool below the falls and the one below the road bridge at the weir there is little room for spinning.

FORESTRY HILL LOCHS CAM, EUN and DALACH

Brown Trout   **Season: 15 March - 6 October**

This group of hill loch is strung along the ridges of the Inverliever Forest about 2 miles from the loch side road. For the fishers who would like to be on their own with little chance of company this is the place for you. Best from early May on and again in September the trout are typical in as much as anything from 6oz and up can be expected with diligent thoughtful casting a good breakfast should be had of keepers (over 8in) all for the paltry sum of £2.50 per rod day. **Ford Hotel (01546) 810 237** issue the permits and advises on the route.

See advertisement on page 11

LOCH EDERLINE and ESTATE HILL LOCHS

Brown Trout (Fly only), Pike.   **Season: 15 March - 6 October**

Loch Ederline, just half a mile from the Junction at Ford holds pike of some repute and maybe some other course fish. It is a very scenic location with easy access. The hill lochs are in a group of 18 accessible by private road through the estate. Permit and route information: Keepers House, Tel: (01546) 810 215.

INVERAWE FISHERIES & FISHING HOLIDAYS

Just off the Dalmally/Oban road by Bridge of Awe a signposted road leads to the Estate complex with an exceptionally well stocked home produce shop and Tea Room. The Smokery will more than entertain your palate, glass walls allow one to catch each step in the process of fish smoking and curing. Modernised self-catering holiday cottages with open fire, extra drying facilities and unlimited fishing for up to six fishermen are available on the estate.

RAINBOW TROUT LOCHS - FLY ONLY - OPEN ALL YEAR

Morning/Afternoon	9am - 1pm or 1.30pm - 5.30pm	£13.50
Full day	9am - 5.30pm	£19.50
Evening	6pm - 9pm	£13.50
Father and Son	Half Day	£20.00
Rod Hire	£2.50 per permit	Net Hire £1.50

The three lochs are stocked daily as required. The loch nearest the car park is set in surroundings of natural mature treed country with ample casting space including disabled access. The lochs vary considerably in setting. A short walk (100 mt) over a forest trail and the second loch lies in a small valley with varied shoreline and ample casting platforms. The quiet surroundings and wonderful location are top attractor. The stock fish, held and brought on in sea pens provide exceptional sport and great eating. Records show that returning anglers are certainly pleased with the quality of fishing.

RIVER AWE - INVERAWE & LORN BEATS - Fly Only

Salmon and Sea Trout   **Season: 11 February - 15 October**

One mile of this famous river is available through the estate on weekly lets or day permit. It is usually well into April or even May before there are regular arrivals of salmon or sea trout. For 1997 there is a River/Loch permit at only £25.00 to £35 per day.

FISHING LESSONS

Daily trout fishing lessons at 10am and 2pm Monday through Friday include one hour of instruction and three hours of fishing, includes rod and net hire. Pre booking advised - limit 5 rods. **Cost per rod £25. Tel: (01866) 822 446. See advertisement page 20**

RIVER ORCHY

Salmon & Sea Trout   **Season: 11 February - 15 October**

This river is fortunate to derive some feed from Loch Tulla. Previous to the building of the dam on the River Awe it was one of the greats in salmon fishing. However, there is wonderful news with new runs of grilse which are no doubt the results of the sterling work of the management who have since 1991 been depositing up to 100,000 fry from there own hatchery. The first of these grilse returning increased the returns by 200% above normal in 1995 with grilse to 6lb and salmon up to the middle teens. There are seven beats on the river and rods may be available at about £15 in March to £30 Aug/Sept/Oct. **Loch Awe Stores** in the village of that name on the A85 is well stocked with tackle and has LAIA permits and handles most of the River Orchy permits. Call in, you will find Ken and Frances very helpful. Some weekly lets and self catering cottages in the area are handled by **West Highland Estates Office** in **Oban: (01631) 563 617** who in fact hold fishing, stalking, self catering accommodations and such throughout the West Highland and Islands.

THE AWE FISHERIES TRUST

A short reporting message from Dr. Colin Bull., AFT Biologist.

The awe Fisheries Trust conducts research and monitoring of the fish stocks in and around Loch Awe. Over the past two years, staff have carried out projects aimed at increasing the information on the status of fish stocks, so that future enhancement projects can be attempted.

Surveys have been carried out on the juvenile populations of trout and salmon in the spawning tributaries, the fish stocks in of Loch Awe, Avich and Ederline. The brown trout stocks in both Loch Awe and Avich are large and healthy and although rainbow trout still escape from farms, there is no evidence of spawning by this specie in the catchment.

Angling catches are extremely important in managing any fishery and can provide useful information on the status of particular stocks. Angler on Loch Awe are now being requested to complete and return their catches from both season and day tickets. For further info or to assist the Trust contact: **Dr. Colin Bull, AFT Biologist, Old School House, Ardconnel, By Dalmally, Argyll. PA33 1BW. Tel: (01866) 844 293**

18

PART THREE

LOCH FYNE SIDE AND KINTYRE

At the head of Loch Gilp - a small sea loch which is an extension of the great Loch Fyne - lies Lochgilphead. Views of mountain and loch from the square infer a still rural township which however, has all the requirements of the modern visitor, angler or not. It is a clean wee place and is attractive and hospitable as it was in 1959 when I first visited. **Archie MacGilp,** a died in the wool local who will tie your favourite flies with traditional expertise (ask him about Kerr's Pink) has opened a tackle and country wear shop which is just stuffed with good things for outdoor people. Archie offers trout fly casting instruction on local lochs and issues permits for everywhere. Give him a call at *Fyne Tackle* **22 Argyll Street**. There is plenty of interest in the area, to the north just few miles out the A816 Oban road is Kilmartin Glen the ancient Kingdom of the Scots. *Dunadd* and its world famous footprint where the Kings of Dalriada were crowned is open to public viewing. Just north a few miles is the mighty Loch Awe, but that's a whole other chapter. Forest enterprise of this region are to be congratulated on the many fine walks and picnic areas they have provided, with colour maps and detailed guides available free. East along Loch Fyne side are fine views across to Cowal and beyond as you pass through Loch Gair, Minard, Killean and so to Inveraray. Inveraray, Lochgilphead, Tarbert and Campbeltown all have **Tourist Information Centres** where you can rely on best attention and detailed information. South through Knapdale is Tarbet, a typical fishing village just north of the Kennacraig ferry terminal where **Caledonian MacBrayne** sail to Islay, Colonsay and Oban. To the writers knowledge no casual fishing is available from Lochgilphead to Carradale half way down Kintyre. The B8001 is much more scenic than the main road, hugs the shore of Kilbrannan Sound passing Claonaig where the ferry plies to Arran. Superb views reward taking this coast road down through Carradale to Campbeltown.

LOCHGILPHEAD AND DISTRICT ANGLING ASSOCIATION

Brown Trout - Fly only   **Season: 15 March - 6 October**
Permit: £6 per day - £20 Weekly (Monday - Saturday)

For a pittance, the fisher can enjoy sport on a grand selection of trout lochs which are of very easy access. There are eleven lochs available in the hills which can be accessed by car on the B841 then left as far as the top of the hill above Cairnbaan. From here the walk is on forestry roads to the water of your choice. A sensible map is issued with permits so no compass or boy scout assistance is required. Normally only ten permits are issued daily for the hill lochs so there is infinite space and tranquil ambiance. Typical hard fighting Scottish hill loch trout will give you memorable competition and a fine breakfast. Only fly fishing is permitted. Size 10 and 12 are good in most conditions except maybe for boat fishing when a good wave demands 8s. Productive dressings are Grouse and Claret, any of the Pennells, and Dark Mackerel. No camping or fires are permitted and dogs must be on leash. The following are typical of the lochs in this area. Permits are available from:

Fyne Tackle 22 Argyll Street Lochgilphead Tel: (01546) 606 878

See advertisement page: 19

LOCH-AN-ADD

The loch side parking make this popular and the troot are all about 10in so you get lots of keepers to feed the hungry weans! There have been some nice fish taken recently and though 97' was very dry and hot the good breeze up here produced rising conditions.

LOCH-NA-BRIC

This is the smallish loch to the right of the road about half way along Loch-an-Add and much favoured by the locals who expect reasonable returns for their fishing time! A good day may bring rewards of five or six brownies up to about 3/4lb with good possibility of a heavier fish to 3lb. On the other hand if your a real dumplin' you might swear "there's na' fish in't". Lochs like this need tender loving casting of wee soft dry Heather Moths, preferably in the evening. Ripple or not, your sure to get some mighty fine pulls with this tactic.

GLEAN LOCH and LOCH-NA-FAOILLINN

These lochs are a short walking distance to the east (into the sun in the morning) and are of similar potential with troot of 8 to 9oz the norm. This string of waters on hill and in forest is a wonderful place to spend some time where you can walk from loch to loch easily fishing as many as four or five in a day. As you begin to get a feel for the water, the shade, the sunlight and the breeze you will notice more the wild life. Not least the changing moods of the troot as the breeze shifts the surface and slightest temperature changes pop flies to the surface and activate both fisher and fish.

LOCH COILLIE-BHARR and LOCH BARNLUASGAN
Boats: Collie-Bharr £6 + £5 per rod. Barnluasgan £5 + £4 per rod
Probably the best of the trout lochs in the area these waters fish very well from opening day 15th March right through June with some really fine catches recorded. There is a great May fly hatch with late April into May being the best bet. September can produce the same quality of fish though of course there is always the weather to consider and perhaps this is another loch which would fish better between dusk and dawn. Good drifts are the north bay's the north west bank and the small bay in the south east corner. Most of the banking is heavily wooded and so if the wind is wrong you are stuck with a flat calm. The forestry have opened up a walk round the loch which is a nice place to picnic or to take non fishers and children. Situated in the forest of Knapdale about 61/2 miles from Lochgilphead the lochs are easily reached from the Tayvallich road B8025 and then a left to Garnagrenach where **Archie Macvicar Tel: (01546) 850 210** issues the boat permits. There are three boats, two of which are on Coulibar.

LOCH GLASHAN
Brown Trout   **Season: 15th March - 6th October**
About 3/4 by 1/2 a mile in size this forestry loch offers fine sport for the fly fisher. The inhabitants are of the 8 to 10oz variety but what they lack in weight they make up for in numbers. It is a good loch for small parties or clubs to visit since the forestry have remade the road and provided a parking place just 300 meters from the loch. In the forest of Asknish this is a very scenic location with great forest trails and walks ideal for family picnics while the fishing members cast a line or two. It is into May before sport picks up here with June probably the most productive and then the usual September burst of activity from the wild wee troot. Bank fishing from the east and north banks is the local choice preferably with a south west wind in dull day light. Good flies include Black Pennel, Cinnamon and Gold, Woodcock and Yellow and if its bright try a Butcher. The loch is in the forest above the Glasgow road A83 just 1 mile north of Lochgair. Get your permit first though from **Archie MacGilp at Fyne Tackle in Lochgilphead** for £3.50 a day, otherwise the forestry ranger will be ragein'.

RIVER DOUGLAS - Argyll Estates - Inveraray
Salmon and Sea Trout - Fly Only   **Season: April - October**

Travelling west along the A83 from Inveraray the river is just before the Fourth mile stone. Even not so agile anglers will find that the ease of access and the agreeable situation of this big spate burn make for a pleasant day's sport - always supposing there is enough water running to entice fish from the sea. Perhaps from May, but far more likely June, fish are expected to arrive with July and August the best bet. As usual, if you get it right you could be frying tonight! Permits are £6 per rod day.

HILL LOCHS
Brown Trout   **Season: 15 March - 6 October**

Just behind Inveraray, on the shoulder of Am Buachaille, at about 1,060 ft. is Loch Righeachan and a few lochans. These waters contain brown trout of about 8oz, with specimen of 1lb likely to surprise the angler who has come this far; At Auchindrain, about six miles west of Inveraray on the A83 take the secondary road which cuts inland to the right. After crossing the Leacann Burn on this road a walk of about a mile will bring you to Loch Leacann, or you can just follow the burn up. Wee troot of the 8/9oz size inhabit this loch but you would swear they were 3lb'ers the way they rip line off your reel, do not however be flippant of them! I took a fine 2lb wild trout from this wee loch just a while ago, on a dry parachute, a Badger, size 14, from Dickson's in Edinburgh, in early June. Permits £2.50 per rod day. Argyll Estates Office (01499) 302 203

CAMPBELTOWN
KINTYRE FISH PROTECTION AND ANGLING CLUB
Season: Brown Trout 15 March - 6 October
Salmon and Sea Trout 15 February - 31 October

This is a very well organised club with sound goals successfully providing excellent loch and river fishing with modest permit fees for visitor and local alike in the Campbeltown area. The lochs provide brown trout fishing which usually become active from April right through June and then again in September. Salmon and sea trout from July on in the burns and rivers are of course spate activated, hence the expression "if you get it right - its Magic". Regulations are no more than would be expected, Fish under 9in to be returned, No fires and No dogs and please observe the Country code of courtesy and consideration of others and their property.

The majority of the waters are Fly Only with the exception of Loch Cross-hill (now stocked with steelheads - see separate entry) and Southend River where spinning is permitted and worm in the river in spate conditions. Campbeltown Association Permits are well laid out with clear regulations and are issued at two Tackle dealers: A. P. McGrory Tackle, Tel/Fax: (01586) 552 132 and Donald Kelly's Country Sports Tel: 01586 522 822 **Permits: (1998) Day rod £3, Weekly £12.**

CONIEGLEN WATER - NO SUNDAY FISHING
Though there are some good pools the length of this river it is very much spate activated and should be judged accordingly. While spinning is allowed worm may only be used in spate conditions. Salmon and sea trout are expected from mid July with water and there are some resident brownies should the fancy take you. The club section is both banks from Pennygowan to Southend. The B842 runs parallel with the river so access is simple. Favoured local spots are behind the wee St Blaan's church and down at the estuary with a falling tide.

GLEN BRECKERIE WATER   NO SUNDAY FISHING
A small stretch of the upper river known as the "AMOD" beat can be fished on the Conie Glen permit but is not given the same attention due to tricky access. Take the B842 to Southend, continue past Keil Hotel then South Carrine, take the Campbeltown road on the left at 200 yards to Amod at about three miles. One of my "must fish again" Kintyre rivers I took three sea trout totalling just short of 9lb in July 1967 on a **size 10 Dark Mackerel**. Only a 1/2 mile long it is interesting water and well worth a cast or three.

MACHRIHANISH BURN   NO SUNDAY FISHING
Running into the Atlantic six miles west of Campbeltown where the sands of Machrihanish attract so many visitors this wee burn in times of spate attracts every fishing fanatic from six to whatever in the area. It was free to fish in 1959 and maybe still is! Just a burn by any standard it appears there is still a large head count of salmon run the gauntlet with some success otherwise they could not keep up the performance so long! Its the worm that takes most fish but there is room for skilfully fly or spinning if you have a mind. July through September is the best bet.

LOCH LUSSA - No dogs - No fires   NO SUNDAY FISHING
Two miles long and about a half mile across this man made reservoir sup-
plies a local Hydro generating station. A **fly only** water which was previously stocked with both rainbow and brown trout it is now totally inhabited
by the brownie. Served by a normal county road signposted **Gobagrennan,**
which branches from the A83 just north of the town and leads directly to
the dam and then as far along the west bank as the club boat house though
no boats are available for hire. The east shore can be accessed by crossing
the dam at the south end. There is no track along the shore but it is easy
walking. In times of low water great care must be exercised due to infirm
peat hags and silt beds throughout the loch. This is a very rural region with
plenty of fauna and flora visible to the quiet observer. The native residents
are of the 8 to 12oz variety and have been of that constancy for the last
thirty five years when the last rainbow was caught. There is usually at least
a light breeze up here which assists our angling efforts to a degree. Popular
local flies are Kingfisher Butcher, Blae and Black, Black Spider, Zulu, and
Grouse and Claret. My cast, in daylight, would carry a Bluebottle Spider
and or an Olive Dun and from late July **a** rather over fed **oatmeal Heather
Moth** dry would be the one to bring home the breakfast.
LOCHS AUCHALOCHY (Fly Only) and RUAN
These lochs covered by the same permit so there is fair choice and time
to change your mind for weather or any other reason. They are of easy
access just north of the town. There is no car access to these lochs but
they are only a mile from the town, the path is safe, so just take your
time. A farm track leaves the A83 just out of town and you walk this
taking the left hand branch at the Y junction, continue up the hill and
Auchalochy appears on your left or continue just a wee bit and there is
Ruan. Trout in both lochs are similar at the 8/9oz mark with fish of less
than 9in being returned. As is usual the larger fish are frequently seen
moving but no exceptional returns have been made of late. South facing
lochs which have a degree of protection from cold easterlies they have a
reputation of being early starters. There is good underwater plant life
with a little bother to the angler as it thickens only at the north end in
summer. Butcher, Green well, Wickams Fancy and Zulu are the favoured
local flies. Spinning is permitted on Ruan only.

CROSSHILL RESERVOIR

Part of the town water supply this water is situated south of the town by about one mile. Take the B842 for Machrihanish, just past the creamery turn left up Tomaig Road, continue up the hill to a sharp right hand turn, take the farm track signposted Crosshill Farm where you must get permission to park. Stocked with Steelheads in 1998 it gave great sport and was very popular and good value fishing. At this time (January 99 there is still a question mark on further stocking! **A separate permit is required.** There were lots of wee trout in this loch which had the reputation to be "Bonnie Fechters". However, it remains to be seen if they survive the Steelheads! Its a good place to take family and kids for a picnic. **Permits are: £10.00 per rod day with a 3 fish limit**

GLEN LUSSA WATER

About 41/2 miles from Campbeltown on the Carradale B842 road is the village of Pininver where the Lussa enters the sea powered as it is by the outflow from the Hydro generating station. Privately owned the stretch available is both banks from Glenlussa House to the sea with day permits issued by the bailiff at the riverside. Fish arrive from late June and in July night fishing is permitted for sea trout only. It appears that spinning and worming is permitted at the discretion of the bailiff.

RIVER CARRADALE - CARRADALE ANGLING CLUB

Salmon & Sea Trout   **Season: 1 May - 31 October**

This club water which is readily available by visitor permit can with the required spate conditions provide good sport with sea trout from June and salmon from July. There is a lower section where any legal method is permitted and from the Dippen Bridge upstream it is **Fly Only** and spinning in waters above the 31/2ft mark. There is some good fly water when in condition and the writer found that an 11ft sea trout rod was the ideal instrument here. You do require waders since fishing it properly requires crossing the river several times. Productive flies for Salmon are Shrimp, Stoats Tail and Jock Scott in size 4 to 8 and Invicta, Grouse and Claret and Dark Mackerel in 8 and 10 for sea trout. Carradale village has a hotel, a store at each end of the village, plenty of B & B and a garage which issues permits at the pier. Day permits are £5, weekly £12 and just £18 for a month. Country Sport of Campbeltown also issue permits for this water.

TANGY LOCH
Brown Trout   **Season: 15 March - 6 October**

A privately owned loch the club leases the fishing and previously made permits available to visitors. The loch is situated off the A83 on the west coast of Kintyre. About fourteen miles north of Campbeltown is a farm road signposted Tangy, follow the road to the telephone box, continue straight ahead up the track for 150 meters and turn right to the farm. There is a good head of trout here and they are of very good quality coming into condition early and fishing right through the season. There is some weed problems by mid summer which require skilful casting to avoid. This is **Fly only** and some of the taking dressings are **Red Soldier Palmer, Greenwell, Cinnamon and gold and Invicta. It seems this loch may not be available in 1999 – inquire locally.**

LOCH CIARAN
Brown Trout - Fly Only   **Season: 15 March - 6 October**

This 160 acre loch is in the hills about two miles above the village of Clachan about eleven miles south of Tarbert. It appears to have a good head of native brownies and has not been fished much in the last few years. There is a private forestry road to about 50 meters of the water which is limited to bank fishing. Being quite high on the hill it will be into mid April before things warm up enough for the troot to become hyper active. I would think this could be a good loch in May. There is forestry plantation surrounding some 40% of the loch but no problem with access or casting Permits are £4.00 per day from the Clachan shop or at Donald Kelly's Country Sports in Campbeltown

The guides most Scottish anglers refer to
FISHING SCOTLAND
ROSS & CROMARTY - SUTHERLAND & CAITHNESS

INVERNESS-SHIRE ISLE OF SKYE MORAY & NAIRN

FROM TOURIST INFORMATION CENTRES, TACKLE SHOPS, SPORTING HOTELS OR FISHING SCOTLAND

Welcome to Campbeltown

*The Management and Staff extend a warm welcome to you.
Whatever you want from your holiday, be it a relaxing leisurely
stay or a golfing or fishing break, perhaps you enjoy bird-
watching or just chatting to friendly people whilst enjoying the
superb scenery, there is something for everyone. Lovely walks
and beautiful beaches.*

PERMITS FOR SALMON, SEA TROUT &
BROWN TROUT AVAILABLE LOCALLY

THE ROYAL HOTEL
2 MAIN STREET, CAMPBELTOWN
ARGYLL PA28 6AG
TEL: (01586) 552017 FAX: (01586) 553116

COT HOUSE SERVICES

COT HOUSE - DUNOON - ARGYLL - PA23 8QT
Tel: (01369) 840 333 Fax: (01369) 840 710

Your one stop Petrol Station - Shop - Off Sales on the A815 just one
hour from Glasgow five miles north of Dunoon

**The Farm Snack Bar & Licenced Restaurant seats 70 and
welcomes any order from tea & coffee to a 5 course meal.
Coach parties welcome.**

TROUT & SALMON FISHING
Permits for a half mile stretch of the Little Echaug
Season: May - October
Limited permits at £6.00 per rod day - NO SUNDAY FISHING

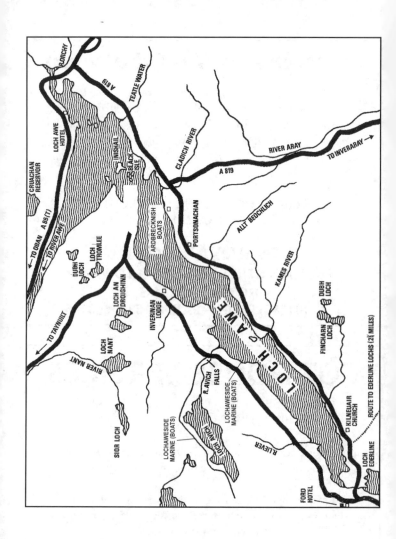

PART FOUR

COWAL & DUNOON

The five fingers of scenic landscape of this undiscovered corner of Argyll have deep fiord like blue watered sea lochs reaching far into the heart of the Cowal peninsula. Rich in heritage, fascinating in natural environment, fabulous scenery and with an interesting climate almost a world of its own. There is a feeling of being on an island such is the road system which hugs the shores, but also affords wonderful access to numerous quiet glens and attractive villages and roadside hotels. The famous Cowal Highland Games held every August in a setting which takes some beating should not be missed, its spectacularly home grown "SCOTTISH" entertainment and hospitality. The newly opened and redesigned **Hafton Hotel** is set in wonderful mature grounds on the edge of Dunoon with exceptional views over the loch to distant hills. Getting to Cowal gives you the choice of driving the A82 to the A83 and turning of at the Rest and Be Thankful on to the B828 hill road for Lochgoilhead and Hell's Glen or stay on the A83 a few miles and take the A815 to Strachur and Dunoon or branch to the B8000 (my own Favourite) which meanders down by Castle Lachlan, Otter Ferry and Kilfinan in scenic Highland grandeur by Portavadie where a **Caledonian MacBrayne** ferry plies back and forth to Tarbert on Kintyre. If your in a real hurry to get to Cowal with or without a car the **Caledonian MacBrayne** drive on drive off ferry shuttles back and forth from Gourock from dawn till dusk. Interlaced with fine quality country roads you could spend a lot of time on Cowal and that's before you start considering the fishin'. Which brings us to the very subject of this wee book. There is quite a selection of brown trout, sea trout, salmon and rainbow fishing available. **Purdie's 112 Argyll street, Dunoon** should certainly be your first stop, for it is here that Mr & Mrs Purdie dispense the permits on behalf of the local association and are well able to give you current strength or otherwise of the fishings. They also carry all manner of fishing tackle and an extensive range of quality country clothing. Regarding accommodation, eating out, cruises, tours and all the good things you should not miss out on, visit the **Tourist Information Centre** on **Alexandria Parade Tel: 01369 703 785** overlooking the Firth of Clyde.

DUNOON AND DISTRICT ANGLING CLUB

If you have to contend with overcrowded conditions on your home waters! Like you can see three other anglers while you are casting? You really have to get away and spend a wee while with us. Within 15 miles of Dunoon there is Wild Brown Trout fishing that people write books about! Then there is salmon and sea trout to consider. The scenery and lack of commercialism will unwind you so quick you might even start visiting the estate agent. The catch returns are at last rising after some shortage in passed seasons and if one organises to fish "late and spate" you could be offering smoked salmon to your visitors next Christmas. A rainbow fishery run and stocked by this enterprising club ensures there is always quality fish to stalk even if nature runs the rivers low and the loch brownies are in a dour mood. All the usual Scottish selection of flies will take troot on occasions, but, I have noticed a reluctance of some fishers to go down to wee 14 and 16s from June on. **Wee flees** are magic attractor of Wild troot in both the coldest and warmer times of the season. Dressings the writer has found productive here include **Dark Mackerel (Traditional dressing of wool, not lurex), Grouse and Claret, Teal and Green, and Invicta.**

A seven consecutive day **'ALL WATERS'** permit at £40 for adults and £20 for accompanied under 16s (Maximum of two per adult) is available in limited numbers from 1 May though 15 October. Visitors should check availability well in advance at **Purdie's Tackle Shop 112 Argyll Street Tel: 01369 703 232.**

LOCH TARSAN   **Sunday fishing permitted**
Brown Trout - Fly Only   **Season: 1 April - 30 September**
Bank: £7 per day £21 per week - Boat: £10 per day + deposit

This is the "Jewel in the Crown" of the Association and enjoys considerable reputation with both visitors and locals. Located on the B836 in Glen Lean just eight miles north west of Dunoon this large 340 acre Hydro loch is stocked with high quality brown trout which can be stalked from the bank or by traditional boat fishing. Many locals prefer bank fishing and certainly show consistent returns. The loch is well fed by river and run off and is best favoured in May, June and September particularly in overcast breezy conditions. This is an ideal place for a family picnic in safe wilderness surroundings.

LOCH LOSKIN
Brown Trout - Fly Only Boats £10 per rod - 3 fish limit per rod
It is Boat fishing only here and they should be booked ahead of time especially from late April through June and again in September when the troot are most active. A very good head of fish is retained by regular stocking with at least 11in quality trout. Fish of less than 10in are returned. This is a wee loch, should be lochan! And lends well to traditional boat fishing. Being as it is only a mile from Dunoon town centre out the A885 Sandbank road it gets a lot of attention from the 'sudden impulse' fisher. A bit of a bonus here is the September sea trout run which can add some spice if you strike right.

DUNOON RESERVOIR   Sunday fishing permitted
Rainbow Trout Fly only   Season: All year
Bank fishing only: £11.00 per day £35 per week 5 fish limit per day
At the head of the Bishop's Glen, only a short walk from Dunoon Main Street this well stocked rainbow fishery previously held a good stock of brownies of which the writer has heard no reports recently! The very clear part peat bottomed water is stocked with up to 6lb rainbows, is of very easy access with pleasant bank fishing where both the fishing and non fishing attendance is uncrowded and inviting as another safe and pleasant picnic spot. The quality of fishing is excellent and a five fish limit is most reasonable at such modest charges. The road to this former town water supply is narrow and requires great care and consideration of the walking public, additional to other vehicles.

The season on all club Rivers is: 1 May - 15 October
Any legal method permitted for Salmon, Sea Trout & Brown Trout

RIVER MASSAN   Permit: £7 per day
Just six miles north of Dunoon on the A815 the Glen Massan road branches to the left just before Orchard, and runs very close to the river for almost six miles. The fishing extends from a board about 3/4 of a mile north west of Stonefield farm downstream to the confluence with the River Echaig just short of the estuary. Though the majority exercise the right to fish worm or spinner there is some nice fly pools on the upper reaches. This is a very scenic area with beautiful views, the fact that recent returns have improved should be looked on as a bonus.

RIVER CUR   **Permit: £7 per day £21 per week**

Fishing extends from Loch Eck, on both banks, to 600m above the bridge at Glenbranter. Fishing is prohibited however on the west bank from Glenbranter bridge upstream for 40m to Bridgend Cottage land and from the bridge downstream to the Glenshellish burn and 300 m beyond. Access is from the A815 near the 14th mile stone from Dunoon Pier, take the forestry road down the west bank where the river flows into Loch Eck and from the footbridge over the Glenbranter Burn. The main pools are very easy of access with perfectly good fly fishing when a spate is running off. Any legal method. No maggots.

RIVER FINNART   **Permit: £6 per day £21 weekly**

A typical West Highland spate river which flows into Loch long just north of Ardentinny some 12 miles from Dunoon on the A880. Extending from the estuary upstream for about 1 3/4 miles to the bridge leading to Craighoyle farm this big burn has very good returns of sea trout and the occasional salmon. Again mainly worm and spinning is exercised here yet there are some sections which lend themselves to the fly at the right time of run off. Any legal method. No maggots.

RIVER RUEL   **Permits occasionally available: £12 per day**

Some one mile of single, right bank fishing, which is fly only water and stretches from the Camquhart Farm stone wall, downstream to the bridge carrying the Glendaruel to Otter ferry Road. This is about 17 miles from Dunoon on the A886. This stretch is only a couple of miles from the sea, so if you get the spate right you could be adding to the improved returns of the last few seasons. Fly and high water spinning. **NOTE: These waters are regularly patrolled by Bailiffs. Poachers have been and will continue to be prosecuted.**

RIVER GOIL (Angling Club Water) No Sunday Fishing
Salmon and Sea Trout   **Season: 14th March - 31st October**

This river, owned and managed by the club since 1988. Four netting stations were purchased in 94' and their control is a major plus to the fish entering the river. Access is very good, the B828 which leaves the A83 at the Rest and Be Thankful is never more than a short walk from the river which provides just over five miles of fishing through Glen Mhor before it enters the sea. With its considerable catchment area this spate river should provide good fishing conditions from June on and certainly from July with returns indicative of a larger stream. Fish are taken throughout the system which has 18 productive pools. Fly or worm are the permitted methods, locally favoured flies are Teal Blue and Silver and Shrimp in size 10. This is a very scenic area and except at the very lowest and higher parts of the glen is very suitable for picnic outings with children. No dogs or fires are permitted. A thirty member club on occasions there is availability of membership. Inquiries and permits: The Shore Inn, Lochgoilhead. Tel: (01301) 703 340 Day permits (2): £15, Weekly £50.

COT HOUSE SERVICES - LITTLE ECHAIG FISHING
Just five miles north from Dunoon on the A815 this one stop service station, snack bar, restaurant and shop have a 1/2 mile stretch of the Little Echaig River, a spate stream, which has good reputation for salmon and trout when there has been a bit of fresh rain and the river is running off. The fishing is close by and of easy access. Spinning and Fly are permitted. Any freshet from May through October can bring the fish in. **Permits: £6.00 per day rod. Tel: (01369) 840 333**
See advertisement page 29

H A F T O N
H O T E L

DUNOON • ARGYLL • PA23 8HP

Situated amid mature hardwoods and spacious lawns on the edge of Dunoon. The hotel enjoys extensive views over the Firth of Clyde with the Highland mountains beyond.

The hotel, completely refurbished for the 1998 season has 26 en-suite rooms, two of which are ground floor with full disabled access as is the dining room and bars.

- INDOOR HEATED SWIMMING POOL
- LUNCH & DINNER SERVICE
- ALL DAY CASUAL BAR MEALS
- GOLF JUST MINUTES AWAY
- PONY TREKKING LOCALLY
- SEA FISHING TRIPS ARRANGED
- LOCAL BROWN TROUT FISHING

- SELF CATERING LODGES

- OPEN ALL YEAR

The resident proprietors *"the Dodds family"* will ensure a warm welcome and service to make your holiday just that much more special.

PLEASE CALL (01369) 706 205
OR FAX (01369) 706 845
FOR THE 1999 BROCHURE AND TARIFF

DUNOON - ARGYLL - PA23 8HP

36

PART FIVE

ISLE OF ARRAN

The picturesque island of *Arran* lies in the firth of Clyde some 14 miles off the mainland and Ardrossan where most visitors embark the Caledonian MacBrayne ferry for the 55 minute sail to Brodick the largest village on the island. A second popular method of travel to Arran is the Clonaig to Lochranza drive through ferry also operated by Caledonian MacBrayne. The Highland scenery of the northern half of the island is dominated by Goatfell 2,866ft (881mt). Compare that rugged aspect with the southern green fields and softer moorland you will understand why 'Scotland in miniature' is so appropriate.

Brodick has a castle and Heritage Museum which should not be missed. However, if you require solid information or assistance of anything local call at the **Tourist Information Centre** at the Pier **Tel: (01770) 302 140/401**. The remains of a 14th century castle which overlook Loch Ranza is said to be where Robert the Bruce landed from Ireland in 1306. Kinloch Hotel at Blackwaterfoot is just a cast down the road from Port-na-Lochan fishery now in its fifth successful year with fly and bait fishing for rainbow trout. The Kinloch Hotel issues permits and rod hire service from 9am every day. Kildonan Castle overlooks the Kildonan Hotel and self-catering complex on the southern most point of the island and Whiting Bay, is a great sea fishing departure point where charter boats, tackle and permits are available from Bay News. Throughout the island there are ample opportunities for walks on well-marked paths through glen, mountain pass, moorland and gently rolling hills. There's a special cycle track of 11 miles from the outskirts of Lamlash to Kilmory. Time is in plentiful supply on Arran! Come on, it's closer than you think.

ARRAN ANGLING ASSOCIATION

Originating in 1942 when the late Duchess of Montrose suggested that the locals form a group to manage the islands burns the aims are to protect and provide reasonably priced fishing for locals and visitors. In conjunction with the Arran Salmon Fishery Board a hatchery was built and became operational in 1993 annually providing native stock fish for the burns. From the 1998 season Association membership has been available to visitors at only £30.00 per annum to fish all AAA waters.

Annual Membership £30 is open to non residents from 1999
Loch Garbad £5.50 per day - Limit of 2 trout per day rod
All rivers - excluding SLIDDERY £7.50 per day - £40 per week
All river - including SLIDDERY £10 per rod day - £50 per week
Juniors (16 and under) half price
Brodick Tourist Information Centre Tel: 01770 302 401

Jimmy the Barber, Lamlash; Kilmory Post Office; Bay News, Whiting Bay; Corrie Golf Club; Kildonan Hotel; Auchrannie Country House Hotel.

LOCH GARBAD Season: 15 March - 6 October

A good 40 minute walk from the main road (there is no vehicle access permitted) partly on farm track, partly forestry path the first impression on arrival being glad the effort was made, such are the sights and sounds of isolation and an overwhelming sensation of peace from first sight of this little loch. All the usual Scottish loch flies are OK here with observant attention to what is hatching being the best advice. Best thing is to be dropped off and collected later at the Ballymeanoch glen farm track.

Season: All rivers and burns 3 May - 31 October

SLIDDERY BURN   Limit of 2 salmon/sea trout per day rod

Access to this 8 kilometre long big burn is excellent, the Ross Road never being far from the water. As with all Arran rivers this is a spate river relying on rainfall to offer continual freshets if any sort of reasonable fishing condition are to be expected. From the headwaters the river tumbles its way south to enter the sea on the south west corner of the island. There is no reason that you cannot fish the fly, particularly at the estuary area or on the upper reaches where there are a few pools where tempting flies could have a field day in falling water. Mostly these fish are from 5 to 9lb with the odd heavy sea trout at the back end clocking 13lb.

LAGG BURN

Starting life as it does, 7 kilometres from the west coast in the heart of a forest, the Lagg, unlike the Siddery burn takes a more leisurely course as it meanders to the sea just below the village of Lagg. There are two very good pools between the main road bridge and the sea which are very worth while. If you are prepared to travel light and hike the 3 kilometres up the burn to what are among the best pools on the island. Races, Bench and Ace pools are all quite long, deep and for 99 percent of the time are disturbed only by deer and other wild life.

SOUTH SANNOX BURN

Glen Sannox is one of the most majestic on Arran and the South Sannox Burn adds much to its beauty with tumbling waters splashing over granite rock formations and through some very fine fishing pools on its journey to the sea just below the road in Sannox Bay. The water is, except in times of heavy spate when it takes just a taint of colour, crystal clear and pure as water comes. An impassable waterfall drops into the 'Mine' pool where beautifully marked brown trout, sea trout and the occasional salmon are the quarry. This lower burn is generally fast flowing and turbulent, best suited to worming with the exception of the tidal stretch which is open.

NORTH SANNOX BURN

From where it crosses the road just half a mile north of Sannox for its short run to the sea the North Sannox burn runs parallel to the road and is of easy access. A peaty watered spate burn both brown and sea trout are residents of the frothy pools where on damp summer evenings the air is filled with the pungent scent of bog myrtle which grows profusely in this area.

Camping, fires, and dogs are PROHIBITED at ALL fishings

RIVER IORSA - Dougarie Estate Water

One of the major rivers of the island, there are two beats, the upper includes boat fishing on Loch Iorsa which by mid June should hold sea trout and salmon assuming there has been a spate. 4 rods are available at £28.75 assuming the weekly rental at £146.87 has not been taken. Further details: Dougarie Estate. Isle of Arran Tel: 01770 840 259

MACHRIE RIVER - FLY ONLY - Season: 10 June - 19 October

Extending 3 miles into the west coast of the island this is the Big river of the island and enjoys a good reputation for both sea trout and salmon fishing. It is a spate river and while its size and catchment assure it comes into condition quickly with a freshet, the fact remains that a long drought is the cross that must be carried by the fisher. There are 3 beats with 2 rods which are changed every day so allowing each beat to be fished 2 days by each rod. Fishing is from the right bank except the 2 top pools and the bottom 3 below the road. Though offered as weekly lets, day rods are on occasions available. There is also a worm fishing section which is available by day permit. Sea trout have averaged 2.51lb and salmon/grilse 6.87lb over the last 5 years with the last two returns being: 78 Salmon/Grilse and 22 Sea Trout in 94' and 34 Salmon/Grilse and 15 Sea Trout in 95'. Charges (1998) were:

Per rod week 10/6-20/7 £106; 22/7-17/8 £143; 19/8 - 19/10 £169;
Per rod day   £25;   £28;   £38;
Worm area   £25;   £28;   £38;

Day and Worm area permits may be obtained from the Water Bailiff, Riverside Cottage, Machrie, Isle of Arran Tel: 01770 840 241. For weekly lets and information Contact: S. J. E. Boscawen, C/O 10 Leysmill, By Friockeim, Angus, Scotland DD11 4RR. Tel/Fax: 01241 828 755.

PORT-NA-LOCHAN FISHERY - Rainbow Trout

Constructed in 1993 this is the first 'put and take' on the island. Located at Kilpatrick, just a mile from Blackwaterfoot the setting is exceptionally attractive with lovely views over Killbrannan Sound and a good chance of a decent breeze to break the surface due to the proximity to the sea. Fed by spring and burn water there is ample through flow to keep the lochans refreshed and the fish active. The trout are from 1 to about 8lb. Bait fishing (no spinning or ground bait) is permitted Tuesday and Thursday from 2 till 4PM in the smaller of the two lochans while the larger is reserved as Fly only, wet or dry. No wading is permitted or indeed required such is the design of the lochans. A catch and release permit is available and for the sudden impulse angler tackle hire is available. The fishery is open every day of the year 9am till dusk. Tackle/permits are also available from Kinloch Hotel. Tel: 01770 860 444 & Bay News, Whiting Bay.

Any 8hrs (4 fish) £18.50 - 6hrs (3 fish) £14.50 - 4hrs (2 fish) £10.50
Any 2hrs (1 fish) £7.50   Sport permit - Any 4hrs £6.00
Parent & Child (under 16) 4hrs X 4 fish £16.50
Juniors (under 16) less 10% - Rod and Line hire £4

THE ASSOCIATION OF SCOTTISH STILLWATER FISHERIES
World class trout angling

Scotland is the home of world class trout angling in stocked stillwaters and ASSF members provide the pick of the bunch.

Double figure fish are quite common in many waters and fish of five to six pound sizes would not raise many eyebrows!

Member waters, which include all the famous names, are spread throughout Scotland and cater for everyone from the first time angler to the highly skilled specimen hunter. We pride ourselves on the professional way memebers run their waters. The quality of fish and facilities are second to none, the very demanding standards which preclude some fisheries from membership of ASSF.

If you have fished any member waters, you will know well the excellent value for money and quality of fishing that is always available. Most member fisheries actively encourage junior and family participation, often with special discounts and tackle hire.

Check the fishery for membership of ASSF before you book your next fishing outing. That way, you are guaranteed a great day out and some of the best fishing in Scotland - real world class!

For a full list of current member fisheries
please write to:
ASSF List
20 Kelvin Drive, Kirkintilloch,
Glasgow, Scotland G66 1BS
or email: assf@fishing-scotland.co.uk
Visit us on the web:
www.fishing-scotland.co.uk/assf

PART SIX
ISLE OF BUTE

Mr. Bell, the pioneer of steam engines and particularly in regards to navigation, would be very pleased with resultant Caledonian MacBrayne Hebridean and Clyde Ferries that ply their 30 minute journey roll-on roll-off ferry back and forth to the Isle of Bute and its Royal town of Rothesay with cars and passengers from Wemyss bay on the Renfrewshire coast just 45 minutes drive from Glasgow city centre. Anglers armed with equipment , who come to fish Loch Fad's famous trout waters for a day or weekend frequently arrive as pedestrian passengers taking a five minute taxi ride to the loch. There are two tackle shops in town, "Bute Arts and Tackle" and "Fishing Tackle" both of which are well stocked with equipment, bait and issue permits. Built in the Victorian urgency for sea front hotels, gardens and entertainment it is still today very much a town on the water. The **Tourist Information Centre** on Victoria street faces the ferry terminal and is staffed by knowledgeable staff with all the right information to hand and a welcome smile. The entertainment Tradition continues in the Winter Garden and The Pavilion with a variety of live shows and a cinema with daily performances of the latest releases. The Pier is a popular location of sea anglers in summer with boat fishing trips readily available. For the non fisher there are tennis courts at the Meadows and a modern Leisure pool, complete with kids beach area, sauna, solarium and fitness room. **The Commodore Tel. (01700) 502 178, The Ardbeg Lodge Tel. (01700) 505 488 and the Port Royal Hotel Tel. (01700) 505 073** all cater well and specifically for anglers with packed lunches, early breakfasts and freezer facilities. A pleasant island to move round there is open access to beaches, coastline and lochs. At the north end of the island is Rhubodach where a five minute journey on the Caledonian MacBrayne drive through ferry shuttles to Colintraive across the Kyles of Bute. For those who like grand buildings and gardens Mount Stuart should not be missed. Plan to spend a day on this spectacular estate, touring the great house and gardens deserves that. There are plenty of perfect picnic sites within the grounds in garden or on shore.

LOCH FAD - FLY ONLY
SEASON: 1 MARCH - 30 NOVEMBER
BROWN TROUT & RAINBOW TROUT

Day Permit: £14.00 (10 fish)   **OAP £9.00 (6 fish)**
Evening/half day: £9.00 (6 fish)   **OAP £6.00 (4 fish)**
Junior: Day £6.00 (4 fish) Evening/half day £4.00 (2 fish)
Boats: Week day £6.00 - Sat/Sun £8.00 All boats have 4HP. motors
Evening/half day: Weekday £3.50 - Sat/Sun £5.00

Opening day on Loch Fadd 1998 provided a real change in the weather of the winter which had been mild and mainly dry. Heavy showers of snow were interspersed with flat calm and produced 254 fish to a total weight of 466lb. 15oz. from 65 rods, so there!

The changeable weather of March was to be the set for the season and you would not believe how good the catches continued. Spring fishing produced some really good stuff. Messrs. Crawford and Costello had 20 fish to 32lb.15oz. and Crawford senior and junior followed that with 15 fish to 26lb.7oz.

The taking flies early on were Orange Gold Head, Black Zonker, and Viva.

The drought of 1987 was forgotten as the wet weather of 98' set records, the burns were in full spate into Fad and the fish just kept on feeding. "Dog" days were few and far between, hatches occurred daily with superb rises right through the season providing incredible fishing at the south end in the shallows.

There were fewer that the normal number of large brownies with 5lb 8oz. the best and the rainbow champ hit the scales at 17lb.4oz. Most fish were taken in the margins in summer and fell to Brown Zonker, Brown Fritz, Damsel Nymph, Stonefly Nymph, Orange Fritz and Dunkeld.

Best of Autumn fishing was at the shallows at the causeway end of the loch where Black Zonker, Black & Green Fritz, Ace of Spades and Green Tag Ace of Spades produced the breakfast.

A BOAT TROUTMASTER WATER

With 175 acres of prime fishing, 30 boats all with 4HP. motors, several stocking each week and the expertise of the staff! Little wonder Loch Fad is the envy of most fisheries. **See inside front cover for information & details of booking or Tel: (01700) 504 871**

Enjoy Super Fishing in Beautiful Surroundings

Limits of fishings
Falls Pool
Falls Gate
Otter Pool
Chest Po
Little Crooked Pool
Big Crooked Pool
Black Pool
Tele
Lower Falls Pool
Mill Pool
Englishman's Pool
Long P
Dog Pool
Shot Pool
Re

The River Garry & Loch Oich

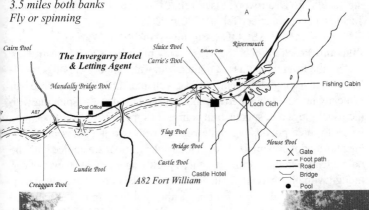

Exclusive salmon fishing on both banks of the River Garry & Loch Oich.

Let by the day or week
Fully fitted cabin
A boat for use on the Loch
3.5 miles both banks
Fly or spinning

Cairn Pool

Sluice Pool

Estuary Gate

Rivermouth

The Invergarry Hotel & Letting Agent

Carrie's Pool

A

Mandally Bridge Pool

Fishing Cabin

Post Office

A87

Loch Oich

Flag Pool

House Pool

Bridge Pool

Lundie Pool

Castle Pool

Creaggan Pool

Castle Hotel

A82 Fort William

X Gate
--- Foot path
— Road
⌒ Bridge
● Pool

LOCH QUIEN

Brown Trout - Fly only   **Season: 15 March - 6 October**

Situated on the west coast of Bute due south of Loch Fad this is a fertile shallow loch in ideal surroundings both visually and as far as access is concerned, the road being only 300mt from the water. Bank fishing is the local favoured method though there is a boat available on occasions. The reputation of the loch is that fish are fast growing and average 1lb at least. The 70 acres holds many much heavier fish, so they say! But, they are very difficult to catch due to the extensive natural feeding available to them. Locally the flies most offered are size 10 & 12s in Mallard and Claret, Black Spider, and Invicta. Day permits are £6 and issued by "Fishing Tackle" 16 Deanswood Place Tel: (01700) 505 062 and Bute Arts & Tackle 67 Victoria street Tel: (01700) 503 598

LOCH ASCOG (Angling Association Water)

Pike and Perch   **Day permits: £2.50 Season £25**

Just a mile from town this the main island water supply provides excellent course fishing with plenty of Pike well into the 20lb class. Dead bait is locally favoured with herring and mackerel used most. Spinning with the usual plugs and spoons brings in just as many BIG fish. Specimen Perch to three pounds are quite regular with two pounders more frequent. Maggot or worm fished on the feeder or float are choice with the pole effective in the warmer weather. A few Roach are taken every year, though with little certainty. The Isle of Bute Pike Group have given considerable time and effort to improve the environment of the loch and ensure future pike stocks. Permits from "Bute Arts & Tackle" and "Fishing Tackle" in Rothesay.

DHU LOCH   **Perch and Brown Trout**

Nestling in the hills above Loch Fad this loch is occupied by a large number of Perch and some Brownies. Access is from the road leading to Fad. Fed by water cuts set in the hills the peat stained run off appears to be ideal and there is talk of it being developed as a fishery! At present its perfect for the angler who likes a quiet location and little company.

GREENAN LOCH Carp, Tench, Bream and Roach

Stocked with course fish this is a very shallow and weedy loch which can be rewarding if you have some little experience and patience to evaluate tactics. All fish should be returned alive so to assist the effort to develop the fishery. Day Permits £1.50 from local tackle shops.

PART SEVEN

ISLE OF MULL

Environmentally and culturally, Mull is one of the richest of the Scottish islands. Afforested, glens, tumbling rivers and sandy beaches offer habitats for red deer, otter, wild goats and even golden eagles, with plenty of room to spare for hillwalkers, fishers and watersports enthusiasts. **Caledonian Macbrayne** make Mull very accessible with car and passenger ferry services from Oban to Craignuir, from Lochaline on the Morvern peninsula to Fishnish and from Kilchoan to Tobermory. The magic begins as soon as you land. Regarded as the capital, Tobermory is a busy wee town with its protected harbour overviewed by the main street with shops, hotels, B & B and restaurants on one side, the activity of fishing boats, dive boats, yachts and harbour industry on the other, just a street breadth away. The **Tourist Information Centre Tel: (01688) 302 182** on the dockhead is ready and able to assist and point you in the right direction. There are two sources of tackle and permits on the Main Street. Brown's (01688) 302 020 is an emporium of ironmongery, hardware, wines, spirits and beer, golf tickets and club hire, fishing tackle and issues **Tobermory Angling Association Permits**. Just a cast along the street **Tackle and Books (01688) 302 366** is stuffed with all manner of reading and art materials, fishing tackle, trout and salmon flies, feathers, sea lures, and local fishing permits and let's not forget the famous **Bridun lures, MADE IN SCOTLAND** here on **MULL** by **KF Tackle Ltd**.

The B8073 which runs round the northwestern extremity of the island provides striking scenic panoramas as it skirts the shores of the trout lochs Mishnish and Torr. Ben More at 3,169ft is the monarch of the island and central in **Benmore Estate** with some of the finest fishing and stalking in the western Highlands. Heading west on the Ross of Mull just before the village of Bunessan a narrow road runs south passed Loch Assapol to **Scoor House (01681) 700 509** where Rosie Burgess has self-catering flats and a cottage in truly rural environment with wonderful views and great fishing. The **Argyll Arms Hotel** in the village of Bunessan is run by Gillie and Duncan MacLeod and is real well suited for touring around the island and it's just down the road at Fionnphort you get the boat to the mystical Island of Iona which has inspired visitors since the time of St Columba, and is the burial place of four Irish, eight Norwegian and forty eight Scottish Kings. Cruises from Iona and Mull to Staffa (Fingals Cave) and the Treshnish Isles are a wonderful experience. Mull is a great place for kids, there is water and sand galore, so come on, don't miss the boat.

TOBERMORY ANGLING ASSOCIATION

With foresight and no doubt with some degree of fortitude! This Association has instigated a management and stocking program of brown trout on the now popular Mishnish Lochs. Charges are modest and reflect the obligation the Association has awarded its management committee in providing good affordable fishing for local and visitor. The associations second location is the Aros Park Lake which requires no stocking such is the escape rate of Rainbow trout from the lake fish farm. There is a 5 fish limit, any under 10in must be returned and NO float tubes are permitted. Bank and boat hire permits from: Brown & Son Tel: (01688) 302 020.

Season: Brown Trout 1 April - 30 September.
Bank Fishing: £10 per day; £30 per week; Under 18s Half price
Boat Hire (2 rods) £5 - 4 Hr; £12 - 10am - 10pm; Permit additional. Boat sessions: 10am - 2pm; 2pm - 6pm; 6pm - 10pm.

MISHNISH LOCHS

The B8073 Dervaig road hugs the shore of these three **FLY ONLY** lochs the habitat of a great number of Brown Trout. Linked together as they are it is a very attractive location visually and interesting to fish. The two narrower lochs have some quite heavy weeding from about mid summer, that however, is the wages of fertile water and a cross that must be carried. From the east end there is a little weed in the first bay which should be of less trouble bank fishing than for boats of which there is one on each loch. Another nice stretch just east of the boathouse where no wading is required looks real interesting. A wooden bridge crosses the most westerly of the narrows and from there the south bank looks the best bet for bank fishing! Doubtless the reason for the bridge. Fish to 4lb have been taken recently which is quite realistic for the size and type of loch and the bi annual stocking of 5" brownies. The abundant food chain ensure these trout do not exactly throw themselves at you, they are however generally free rising. An average day should give you the bag limit of 5, with perhaps two of these pink flesh beauties at 3/4 lb or better. The troot are in good condition by the end of April so any time there is a warm westerly and a wee wave is good for a cast. Popular local dressings are Butchers, Teal and Green, Soldier Palmer, and Grouse and Claret in sizes 10 to 12.

AROS LAKE - Rainbow Trout - No close season

Set deep in the forestry park just on the edge of Tobermory the likelihood of any wind on the surface of this lake is remote. Surrounded as it is with very high mature trees and lots of shrubbery there is little space for other than flicking a spinner. Deep water to the banking precludes wading. There are no casting platforms, so, no fly fishing! Which is a shame. The loch stock is composed almost entirely of escapees from the lake fish farm though it would seem that there will be a further stocking with 1.5 to 2lb. rainbows in 1999. Judging by the dimpled surface any time the writer has visited, it must be one continual great escape. Some very heavy fish have been caught, best to date 10 1/2 lb! There are no boats. A great place for a quiet couple of hours with a good chance of fish for tea.

LOCH FRISA - FOREST ENTERPRISE
Brown Trout, Sea Trout and Salmon

The largest loch on the island this 5 mile long water provides fine baskets of brown trout more than a few sea trout and the occasional salmon and grilse. Access is by forestry road at either end where parking space and boats are located. Lying in a Glen running from the north west and accessed from the B8073 Dervaig road it stretches south east to Aros on the A848. A big burn, the Ledmore River no less, drains from this end into the River Aros the means of migratory fish entering the loch. Trout fishing is better than average with 3/4lb the norm and lots of wee fellows continually tugging to encourage you to strike early when the big one takes! From the Aros end, the road leads along through cleared forest area to the boat and parking area. With easy bank fishing. From the other end the road leads passed the fish farm to the boat location and bank access. Sunday trout fishing is permitted. **No dogs - No fires - Bank fishing £3; Boats: (2 rods)**
 £15, 8am - 4pm or £17.50 till dusk; £5, 4pm till dusk. Boat permits only from Lachie McDowall, Lettermore Farm, Aros. Tel: (01680) 300 436. Bank Permits from: Tackle & Books **(01688) 302 336;** Browns of Tobermory **(01838) 302 020**

RIVER LUSSA - Sea Trout and Salmon.

Flowing from Loch Sguabain in Glen Mar there is in spate condition a run of fish expected from July through September by which time sea trout and grilse could be resident in the many nice holding pools which lend themselves to both spinning and fly fishing. The Tor Ness Falls 3 1/2 miles from the estuary hold up running fish on occasions. Permits for 2 rods daily at £5 each available as for Loch Frisa above.

LOCH DON - GLENNAIN LOCH - AUCHNACRAIG ESTATE
Gleannain Loch - Brown Trout - Fly only

In soft rolling country with sea views over the Firth of Lorn this small loch with easy access for bank fishing is full of small trout of the 2/3 to the pound variety and just rarin' to snatch your fly. Permits are £6 for 24 hours from 8am. A wee rowing boat is £12.

LOCH DON ESTUARY BEAT- Sea Trout

Both banks of the river (big burn) above the road bridge, the pool below the bridge then the south bank only to the sea offer good access to what has been excellent sea trout fishing in 94' with 38 fish between 11/2 and 2 1/2lb recorded in a two week period. 95', 96' & 97' were years of drought. Permits are £12 for 24 hours from 8am. Permits and self-catering details from: Colonel de Klee, Auchnacraig, Loch Don. (01680) 812 486.

BEN MORE SPORTING ESTATE

Fishing on the River Ba, River Coladoir and Loch Ba is frequently available by day permit so providing access to some of the most pro-ductive brown trout, sea trout and salmon waters of Mull. For day permit issue call: **Ben More Estate. (01680) 300 356.** For weekly stalking/fishing lets and accommodation inquiries:
West Highland Estates Office. (01631) 563 617. See advert page 11

LOCH BA

Two thirds of the 4 mile long loch is available for boat fishing, with bank fishing by arrangement. Good runs of salmon can be expected with the first freshets of June. Traditional wet fly is the way to go here with size 8 to 10 dependant on the wave running. Dapping has a strong following and brings up the big fellows. The location is very grand in Highland atmosphere and vision with red deer and eagle likely observant of your efforts. A lunch hut provides for creature comforts. **Boat, engine and fuel for 2/3 rods is £42 per day. Optional Ghillie £53 per day.**

RIVER BA

Some 2 1/2 miles long the entire south west bank from its exit of Loch Ba to the famous sea pool and the many fine holding pools along the way provide more than enough water for the 3 permitted rods to cover at only **£15 per rod**. Though supported by loch run off and a sluice, spate conditions are required to provide ideal conditions to ensure fish through-out the rivers holding pools, of which Bridge, Elbow, Corner, Oak Tree and Drumlang Glyde are the most productive but never miss the sea pool.

RIVER COLADOIR

In the wonderful Highland scenery of Glen Mor which drains into its 6 mile length this river is very enjoyable to fish, with good pools and tumbling cascades where sea trout and salmon can be expected from the first spate of late June. Two beats of the whole north bank alternate at 2pm daily with plenty of room in splendid wilderness country.

See advertisement page 57

RIVER BA - Sea Pool - Killiechronan House Tel: (01680) 300 403
The north east bank of the famous Sea and Rock Pools are available by day permit at £5 per rod. Fly or worm is permitted so with any sort of run off from the river this can be excellent fishing on ebbing tide from June through October. Access is easy, with just a 50yd walk.

TACKLE AND BOOKS - TOBERMORY - (01688) 302 336
The following river and loch fishing permits, tackle and boat rental for fresh water or sea fishing are available from: **Tackle and Books on Main Street. Tobermory**

LOCH TORR - FLY ONLY - Brown Trout, Occasional Sea Trout
Just off the B8073 Dervaig road this beautiful Highland loch is choke fu' of wee broon troot of about 2/3 to the pound and ready to take on any-body wha' dare cast a wee flee in this puddle which was excavated away back in 1899 as what must have been one of the first man made trout lochs. The run out to the sea at the north end permits sea trout to ascend to the loch so be prepared for high drama any time from the end of June.

While any Scottish loch fly might attract the writer found Invicta, Soldier Palmer and Dark Mackerel frequently brought two and on occasions three gluttonous wee trout into action. **Bank fishing is £3 per day, £5 for 2 days or £12 for a week (No Sunday Fishing) Boats are £8 per session, £10 for 2 sessions or £12 all day, 2 rods maximum.**

LOCH SGUABAIN - Sea Trout - Salmon - No Sunday Fishing
Windswept, is a close as English translation gets to name this loch just below the A849 in Glen Mor. It tends to get a wee bit weedy as the season progresses so with a reputation of large sea trout attention to the detail of weed location is important. Traditional wet fly and dapping works well - There is always plenty of wind. Permits and one boat, as above for Loch Tor. Fly. Spinning and bait permitted.

RIVER AROS   Sea Trout - Salmon - No Sunday Fishing
The Aros (a spate river) rises above the south end of Loch Fresa where the Ledmore river from that loch adds value to the Aros for its final short run to the sea at Salen. There are many and varied pools where sea trout and salmon are expected from late June on. The estuary, as is usual on Mull is a well favoured cast and as with the 2 lower beats is FLY ONLY. Small tube flies of the **Hairy Mary or Garry Dog** dressing do well here. Spinning and worm are permitted on the upper beat (Tenga), which is exciting to fish with deep pools and dark runs.
FLY ONLY £12 per day, Estuary only £6.
River Aros Upper Beat: From £10 per rod day, £36 per week.

RIVER BELLART - Sea Trout and Salmon - No Sunday Fishing
Great runs of sea trout and finnock have made this a very popular river with locals and visitors who have experienced the results of a good spate any time from mid June when migratory fish are able to take up residence in the many pools in the glen with easy access from the Dervaig to Salen road. There is an intermittent run of grilse so be ready for serious sport. Try the smaller of the **Bridun spoons (made on Mull)**, they are ideal for searching out small pools and tight channels. Fly, spinner and worm are permitted here. **Day permits are £8 through June, £10 thereafter. two days £15, a week £30. No Sunday Fishing.**
                    See Tackle & Books Advertisement page 48

LOCH ASSAPOL - STOOR HOUSE WATER

James Mckeand is a canny man who likes to talk and participate fishing. Spinning and fly is permitted with **Black Pennel, Peter Ross and Bibio** James own favoured attractors for Brownies and **Teal Blue and silver** for migratory fish. A private road winds up the strath to the glen providing a beautifully secluded environment for hill walking, ornithology and of course fishing. The brownies, free risers, average 2/3 to the pound with perhaps 2 or 3 a day at 3/4 lb and are found to be active from the start of the season on 15 March. Sea trout are expected from May or June with grilse appearing in July. Ferox are known to be in these waters! Deep trolling could produce some surprises. A wee dam was built in 96' to increase the volume of the loch. 4 permits are available for bank fishing at £5 each with the boat another £8 for 2 rods. James, who will Ghillie on occasions, has quality self-catering accommodations very suitable for families. **Tel: (01681) 700 297 See advertisement on page 57**

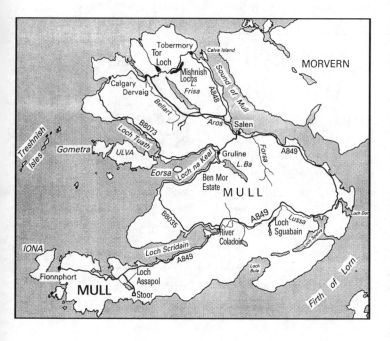

ROSS OF MULL ANGLING ASSOCIATION

Operative from the 1998 trout season the reformed Association has been providing inexpensive day and weekly permits for a number of waters on the Ross of Mull. These waters have been rather under fished of late and in 1998 produced good quality fishing at very reasonable cost.

The waters available by permit are Loch Assapol just a mile east of Bunessan where there is excellent trouting and always the chance encounter with a salmon or sea trout. Loch Poitie is a wee lochan at the roadside about four miles towards Fionnphort where the ferry plies back and forth to Iona. It is well populated with 8 to 10oz. brownies that go bananas at anything vaguely like a fly that happens to enter their domain.

Gillie and Duncan MacLeod at the **Argyll Arms Hotel** in Bunessan offer free trout fishing to residents of two or more days.

Permits are available from the **Argyll Arms in the Village** and cost £10 per rod full day; £5 per half day and £8 an evening session. That's but a pittance ! Just a glance at the scenery is worth more.

PART EIGHT
ISLES OF ISLAY and JURA - TIREE and COLL

'*Jewel of the Hebrides*' was the description the Lords of the Isles used for Islay. Most southerly of the Hebrides, Islay enjoys a mild climate, is 25 miles long by 20 miles across and has for industries, agriculture, distilleries and fishing with tourism growing each season. Islay's charm is elusive. Lush woodlands, bleak grandeur of heather and hill, golden beaches and stark sea cliffs. There are a number of sculptured stones, Celtic Crosses and caves, the ancient remains of the Lords of the Isles castle on the wee island in Loch Finlaggan which is one of the many good trout fishing lochs.

Caledonian MacBrayne ferry services make it easy to get there, with daily service from Kennacraig to both Port Ellen and Port Askaig. The **Tourist Information Centre** at Bowmore **(01496) 810 254** is just waiting your call to send the latest of all that awaits you on these wonderful Highland islands.

Close neighbour Jura, *'Deer Island'* is 28 miles long by 8 broad and close to being divided in two by the sea Loch Tarbert. A good road from the ferry slip at Feolin runs along the eastern shore almost the length of the island leaving the remainder to be explored on foot. Jura offers tranquil walks and hidden beaches with sea and freshwater fishing should the urge take you.

ISLE OF ISLAY - Port Ellen Angling Club

The season for brown trout fishing the club's 5 hill lochs is 1 April till 30 September with May through early July and September being the local choice periods. For 99' day permits are £2.50; weekly £12.00; boats for up to 2 rods £10 per day. Permits and information are dispensed by: **Iain G Laurie, Newsagent, Port Ellen (01496) 302264** The lochs are grouped on the southern Peninsula of Oa and can be reached by four wheel drive vehicle or with walks of only 15 to 30 minutes from the road. Most popular are Kimmabus and Glenastle (upper and lower) with the quality of fish quite constant at about 3 wee troot to the pound. The ferocious affray that follows connection belies the size and would knock the spots of a pound plus stew pot rainbow. Traditional patterns with black and red in the dressing should bring on the action. This is sheep country so dogs must be on lead at all times and no fires.

ISLAY ESTATE FISHING - Fly Only

There are numerous lochs on the Estate with brown trout fishing available by day or weekly permit from 15 March through 30 September. Salmon and sea trout fishing on the Rivers Laggan and Grey can be available at £20 per rod day, however the River Sorn is normally available only by weekly let. As most west Highland spate rivers lack of freshets and run off indicate no fishing. The main lochs are Gorm, Skerrols, Ardnahoe and Loch Finlaggan all of which have boats. Though good fishing and in interesting idyllic scenic locations Loch Laingeadail, Drolsay and Cam are more inaccessible entailing hill walking. Bank permits cover all lochs with the exception of Loch Gorm. All boat charges include fishing permit fee. There is no bag limit, however, Catch returns are an important part of planning and management and failure to make returns here, even for a nil day will result in no further permits being issued to those concerned. **Day permit £3; 3 day £8; Weekly £12; Season £17; Boat (includes fishing permit) £14 per day; £10 per half day from 5pm.** Inquiries and bookings should be referred to: Head **Keeper. Jack Adamson : Tel. (01496) 810 293**

DUNLOSSIT ESTATE FISHING - Fly Only - No Sunday Fishing

Estate fishings consist of 21/2 miles of 3 beats of fine salmon water on the River Laggan upstream from the road bridge on the B8016 and brown trout fishing on 7 lochs, 4 of which are accessible by car, the others are relatively easy to reach on foot.

RIVER LAGGAN - Fly Only

A traditional spate river with the best fishing normally from early July through September. A total of 30 pools are split fairly equally into 3 beats 2 of which are fished from both banks the other from south bank only. A maximum of 2 rods per beat on a daily basis change over at midnight with weekly arrangements also available. Car parking and access is at the bottom of Beat 1 and at the top of Beat 3. A fishing hut is located between Beats 1 and 2. Permits are: £16.50 per day single rod; £55 Single rod 4 days; £60 1 day, 4 rods on 2 beats; £180 weekly, 2 rods on 1 beat. All booking for salmon fishing to Simon Boult (01496) 810 369

Trout Fishing - Fly Only - Season: 15 March - 6 October
Of the 7 available lochs, 6 have boats, Loch Ballygrant has 2, the exception is Loch Bharradail. Though of varied size and location all are indicative of a Highland Island and rural environment. Loch Allan is small and backed by mature estate woods on one side, open country to the other. There is a dam at one end and is a maximum of 15ft deep. Loch Ballygrant is blessed also with wooded and open shore line with the added attraction of several islands which always provide good drifting water. Loch na Cadhan is in surroundings of moorland with splendid views, is very attractive visually and exciting to fish with reed edges, grassy banks and rocky shores with only a 150yd walk to the boat. Loch Lossit is perhaps the most scenic of the estate lochs with two islands to fish round and reflect on history. Loch Bharradail is the boatless loch, has quite reedy shore lines which allows good cover for the fisher on this reputed early loch. Loch Fada is by reputation a summer and evening conditioned loch with very easy close access. Loch Leathann with lovely bays and gravelly shore line has lies throughout and fish perhaps just better than average Highland loch trout. Bank fishing Day permits £3; Boats £10 per day; £5 per 1/2 day except on Lochs Ballygrant, Lossit and Allan which are £13 and £8 respectively during May and June. All trout Permits and information from: **Port Askaig Stores (01496) 840 245**

ISLE OF JURA
Although there are a considerable number of lochs, rivers and burns on Jura it would appear that most of the fishing is retained by the owners.

RIVER LUSS - ARDLUSSA ESTATE - Fly Only
From July through 15 October sea trout and salmon fishing is offered on the River Lussa from the sea up to and including the Loch. Day rods on the river are £25, a boat for 2 rods on the loch £25. The estate has a self catering cottage, with or without fishing or stalking. Information: Charles Fletcher, Ardlussa, Isle of Jura, (01496) 820 323. Ardfin Estate has self catering cottages and good trouting on Market Loch at £5 per day. Information from: William MacDonald (0149) 296 307. Other Jura contacts: Jura Hotel, Craighouse. (01496) 820 243; Jura Stores, (01496) 820 231.

ISLE OF TIREE - ISLE OF COLL

These flat Inner Hebridean crofting islands off the west coast of Mull are noted for their exceptional agricultural fertility. Separated by only a few miles of sea both are serviced by **Caledonian MacBrayne** ferries. Both islands are some 17 miles by 5 at the broadest and are surprisingly well circulated by roads with easy access to the long beaches and cliff scenery. Both islands reveal rich evidence of the past from standing stones to ruined croft houses. It seems however, that at this time no trout fishing is available on Coll. There is a Hotel, B & B, and Self-Catering accommodation available on both islands. Try the **Tourist Information Centre in Oban Tel: (01631) 563 122**

TIREE ANGLING ASSOCIATION - Fly Only

Brown Trout   **Season 15 April - 6 October**

The association has visitor permit trout fishing available including Sundays on Loch a Phuil and part of Loch Bhasapol which has a windsurfing area to the northern end and a bird sanctuary on the western shore. A limit of 9 rods, including local members and a bag limit of 4 trout indicate good management which is also well supported by the returns of 10 members and 18 day permits which show Loch Bhasapol to have produced 234 trout with a .79lb average and Loch Phuil which is not often fished producing 19 trout to average .61lb. The heaviest was 2lb 4oz on a **Black Pennel**. Access to the lochs is good with parking close to the water. Loch Bhosapol fishes best from the south and east banking with no problems. The boat here however seems to be for members only! Maybe there is no demand. Favoured flies include Clan Chief, Soldier Palmer, Lake Olive and Suspender buzzer. Permits are £5 per day; £20 weekly; £30 for 2 weeks; £40 a month; Season tickets are £50 plus a £20 joining fee. Under 16's and over 65's get a 50% discount. Permits from: **Robert Gray, Cruachan, Balenatin, Isle of Tiree PA77 6UA (01879) 220 334.**

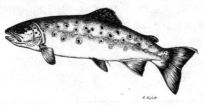

PART NINE

LOCH LOMOND THE 'HIGHLAND FRONTIER'

Such has Loch Lomond aura inspired song and story of scenic beauty, romance, sentimentality and national pride, been expounded to every corner of the earth, it is little wonder Loch Lomond is the most widely known of all Scottish lochs. It is unique in many respects, particularly its location, truly frontier territory and almost within sight of Glasgow City with all that is urban, yet, before travelling half the length of the loch north even a Highlander feels he is almost home. Balloch, Balmaha, and Drymen are rural visitor oriented communities providing bright modern shopping, entertainment and accommodation within sight of woodland walks to tempt you, Loch cruises to relax you, the vastness of blue water and Mountains to impress you, long before you have even made your first cast. For the family, perhaps with non fishers or children in tow, there is no shortage of very accessible beaches and picnic areas, the conservation village at Luss and the Balloch Castle Country Park are only two of the numerous open air attractions to savour without any required physical exertion. Watersports facilities, launch areas for your boat, windsurfer or canoe, nature trails, numerous golf courses and mountains on your doorstep offer new exploration possibilities which ever way you look. On the eastern shore, the one most visitors observe only from across the loch as they travel the main (A82) Glasgow to Glen Coe road is perhaps the first opportunity of travelling a real Highland road. From Balloch, where the **Tourist Information Centre Tel: 01389 753 533** can suggest a new adventure every day for a month and just next door **Sweeney's run regular loch cruises**, take the A811 Stirling road and branch off for Balmaha at Drymen where Lomond Activities specialise in fishing tackle and bike hire. From Balmaha, where **Macfarlane rents fishing and row boats** and issues permits the road continues half way up the loch to end at the **Rowardennan Hotel and self catering lodges** secluded as they are in scenic Highland grandeur with fishing permits and boats available at the hotel. A passenger ferry to the west side of the loch and various loch cruises run daily all summer from the hotel. Walking the West Highland Way (or a part of it) which continues on up the loch side with Fort William its final destination or exploring historic Rob Roy haunts are other alternatives to the attraction of fishing! Or just for a change.

LOCH LOMOND ANGLING IMPROVEMENT ASSOCIATION
New regulations and charges from the end of the 1999 season encourage membership before the year 2000 when the membership will be closed and a waiting list initiated for Membership of the Association. Membership allows one to fish the **River Endrick**, where leased, the **River Leven, River Fruin, Loch Lomond** and parts of the **Gairloch**. Enquires and applications for membership should be addressed directly to:

Loch Lomond Angling Improvement Association
The Secretary - P O Box. 3559 - Glasgow G71 7SJ
Tel: 01417 811 545

An **Entrance fee** of £25.00 (£100.00 from the year 2000)(£12.50 if under18) is payable with first year membership. The annual subscription is in 1999: £137 (£44 if under 18). OAP £59 Must have 10 years of membership. Spouse and children fish the River Leven free when accompanied by member.

NO SUNDAY FISHING - NO GAFFS PERMITTED
SALMON/SEA TROUT MUST BE RETURNED TILL 1 APRIL
For the casual angler short period permits are available:
Loch Lomond & River Leven: £15 per rod day or £40 per week
Under 18's £2.50 per day or £16 season ticket
Season Ticket (local) £63 - Non resident season £76.50

Permits are available locally at Macfarlane & Son Boatyard, Balmaha; Rowardennan Hotel; Tourist Information Centres on Dumbarton Road and Balloch, many Lochside hotels and, tackle shop in Glasgow and surrounding townships and as far east as John Dickson's and Country Life in Edinburgh. **COARSE FISHING :** Roach, Perch and Pike fishing have attained good reputation over recent years with the Pike Anglers Club of Great Britain placing Loch Lomond on the best locations list. Coarse fishing is available all year, **is free and no permit is required.**

LOCH LOMOND AND TRIBUTARIES

Salmon 11 February	**Sea Trout 1 April to 31 October**
Brown Trout	**15 March to 6 October**

No matter what time of year you visit the loch you cannot help but be impressed at its sheer size. At 27.45 square miles in area it is by far the largest fresh water puddle in Great Britain. What is less well known is that Loch Lomond and its tributaries provide excellent game fishing for Atlantic Salmon, sea trout and to a lesser extent the Wild Broon Troot. If one considers however, that most game fishing is carried out at depths of 5 to 10 feet this reduces the area of interest to the angler to a mere fraction of the total size. For fishing, the loch should be considered in two halves, the south end, known locally as the "Bottom End" stretches from Balloch north to **Rowardennan Hotel** where boats, permits and fishing tackle are available, and the "Top End" or "Tap End" from **Rowardennan Hotel** north to Ardlui. The "Bottom End", the most popular area especially during the early and late periods of the season is also the broadest part of the loch where most of the islands and shallower depths are located. Balmaha is the main angling centre ideally situated with easy access to some of the most productive fishing areas. **Sandy MacFarlanes** Balmaha Boatyard rents reliable clinker built loch boats with or without motors at realistic cost and issues LLAIA permits. Serious fishing does not begin until mid March and the first fish usually falls to trolled lures. Locally, Abu Toby spoons of 18 to 20gram, Kynoch Killers, Bridun spoons and Rapala are favourite although there are some who still swear by natural sprat, gold for bright days and the red variety in overcast weather. As the water warms up fly fishing takes over and fishing a team of flies from a drifting boat in anything from size 6 to 10 dependant on the wave running produces great sport from both sea trout and salmon. Yellow flies do well, Mallard and Yellow are almost obligatory on the bob and Invicta on the tail accounts for an awful lot of salmon and sea trout. Other local choice dressings are Woodcock and Mixed, Gold Turkey and Silver and the old reliable Dark Mackerel. Dapping accounts for good numbers of the better fish taken and the bigger the Daddy Longlegs the better, that's for sure. A well favoured drift is across the south side of Inchmoan to a large rock known as Little Ireland. Other productive drifts are the north side of Inchlonaig and the north and west sides of Inchfad. During the warmer weather of July and August fish seem to abandon the shallows and head for the deeper "Tap End" of the loch.

THE RIVER LEVEN

The Leven provides excellent sport for both salmon and sea trout from as early as opening day right through the season. It is fair to say however, that it is usually March before there is any certainty of the "Fish" having arrived in significant numbers. All migratory fish travelling to

Loch Lomond or its tributaries pass through this river from the Clyde. Spinning, bait and fly fishing are permitted except for the **Bonhill Bridge Pool** which is reserved for **fly fishing** only. Spinning in the early part of the season is as would be expected the method that takes most fish. Wooden minnows in Yellow Belly and Brown and Gold share favourite with the Abu Toby spoon. By May the fly fishers are out in earnest mostly with at least 14ft rods and it is no secret that nine out of ten are fishing Ally's Shrimp.

THE RIVER FRUIN (Full LLAIA members only - Fly Only)

This, delightful little river is primarily a back end spate stream which for its size produces some remarkable catches and is very reliable regarding the head of fish which navigate its waters to spawn. When the water starts to drop off after a good freshet the normal procedure would be to start fishing at the upper reaches in the area known as the Meadows and as the water level falls you hop in your car moving downstream where the water is still in good fishing order. As with the loch, yellow flies are the local choice in sizes 6 to 10.

THE RIVER ENDRICK (Full LLAIA members only - Fly Only)

Though a back end spate river the Endrick does not run off as quickly as the Fruin and is in good fishing condition for considerably longer after a good flood. In condition, fishing can be quite excellent and is certain to attract the knowledgable local rods when running fresh. This is the main spawning river for the migrants entering the system and with good water conditions a solid head of salmon and sea trout are resident from mid summer on in the numerous holding pools. Local anglers are always very receptive to visitors and happy to pass on information and location of the **MAGIC** spots.

KILLEARN HOUSE FISHERY

This 2 1/2 acre lochan was landscaped by the proprietors David & Carole Young among mature hardwoods. The outlook is rural with wonderful views of the Campsie Hills. There is a basic fishing Lodge where snacks and basic items of tackle are available and of course toilet facilities.

Fishing hours are 9am to dusk or 10.30pm.

There is sea trout and salmon fishing on a 1 mile stretch of the River Blane available.

From Balloch or Drymen take the A809 for Glasgow, a left onto the B834 Killearn road and the fishery is first right. Tel: (01360) 550 994

STIRLING COUNCIL - ENVIRONMENTAL SERVICES

SALMON CONSERVATION - A DIFFERENT APPROACH

The conservation and sustainability of wild salmon and sea trout stocks are both words that are high on the agenda for angler throughout Scotland at the moment, but what do they mean? For the vast majority of fisheries , on private beats, they mean controllable exploitation of fish by limiting rod and angler numbers with an ability to effectively enforce any additional local restrictions. For a salmon fishery open to the public however this becomes very much more difficult. The control of fishing effort by limiting the number of rods or anglers or charging very high prices to fish discriminates against the ordinary angler. The effective policing of very restrictive local rules also becomes unworkable and ineffective with large numbers of anglers.

Stirling Council has this year pioneered a different approach which uses a set of reasonable local rules together with setting of a catch and remove quota for each angler. The conservation of stock is addressed by restriction on fishing methods integrated with the timing of the various fish runs through the season but in addition have set an annual quota of fish which can be removed from the fishery. This is achieved by issuing each season permit holder with five numbered locking tags. These have to be attached to each fish to be taken away and are threaded through the gills and then sealed before leaving the river. Each tag has a unique number, which is recorded on the permit. This allows the enforcement of rules by bailiffs to be very much more effective and also drives home to the angler that each fish has a high value when taken from the wild stocks. The Council have set a limit of five fish for the 1999 season based on the catch data collected over previous years when 98% of anglers reported a catch of three fish. The scheme no effect on the angler's sport since all other fish are released. This tagging quota scheme is experimental at this stage and applies only to salmon. Quotas will be reviewed annually in line with achieving a sustainable exploitation of stocks into the future.

Further information on the scheme is available from: Tom Dixon, Countryside Management Officer, Room 236, Stirling Council, Viewforth, Stirling. FK8 2ET.   email: dixont@stirling.gov.uk Tel: (01786) 442 936   Fax: (017886) 443 003

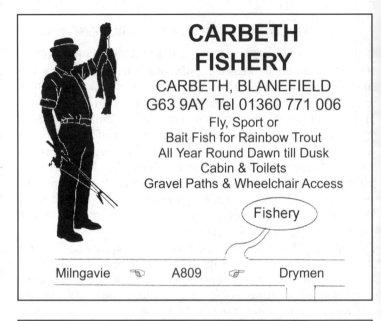

TROUT FISHERIES
BLAIRMORE FISHERY - FLY ONLY - OPEN ALL YEAR

Now with **"TROUTMASTER"** recognition this scenic group of lo-chans is back dropped by mature trees and hidden from the road in a lost valley just off the A811 Stirling - Glasgow road some 2 miles east of Drymen, 20 miles from Stirling and just 17 from Glasgow. The 4 lochans have well grassed surroundings with plenty of room for picnics. There is a natural head of Brownies and the rainbow population is topped up daily with full finned 11/2 to double figure fish. Parking and toilet facilities are just a twenty meter walk from the lochans with a road which should make it reasonable access for wheelchairs. **Day permits are £15.00 x 5 fish; 6hrs. £13.00 x 4 fish; 4 hrs. £10.00 x 3 fish; OAP day £10.00 3 fish; C & R day £8.00, 4hrs. £5.00 Father & Son £20.00 6 fish.** The cabin has rods for hire and serves hot & cold snacks. Rods are limited so booking is advised. **See advertisement on opposite page**.

CARBETH FISHERY - BAIT & FLY - OPEN ALL YEAR

This lochan is 2 acres and stocked with rainbows from 11/2 to 10lb. There are more than a few fish already recorded in at 5 to 71/2lb. The lochan is in a wee valley with very scenic outlook and a good charge of water coming from the feed burn. It is just off the A809 Milngavie/Drymen road about opposite the Carbeth Inn. There's a really great heated lodge with seating, hot meals avail-able, hot & cold water and toilets . The tackle shop has everything including rod rental and live bait. The loch is suitable for wheelchairs with a super easy walkway round the loch. James Rankin the proprietor has picnic and BBQ areas planned for 1999. **Day permits are £14.00 (any 8hrs) 4 fish; £8.50 (any 4hrs) 2 fish; £12.00 Evening 5pm - dusk 3 fish; £15.50 Parent & child 4 fish; Parent & 2 children 6 fish £22.00**
See the advertisement on opposite page

NEILSTON TROUT FISHERY - BAIT FLY - OPEN ALL YEAR

This 14 acre **"TROUTMASTER"** hill loch to the south of the Clyde is so secluded it is hardly believable it is only 11 miles from Glasgow city centre. Bank or boat fishing is available. Additional to quality stocked rainbows from 11/2lb. and up there is a large head of wild brown trout and prime brook trout to keep you occupied. Leave Neilston on Kirkton Road then take a right at the T junction with Springhill Road

which leads directly to the loch. Fishing sessions are very flexible and reasonable and take some beating starting at only **£5.00 for 6hrs. for C & R; 6hrs with 2 fish is £6.50 or £8.50 with 3 fish; All day with 4 fish is £10.00 or £11.00 with 5 fish; Father & Son all day is £15.00 with 7 fish; All have C & R after limit. Boats are an additional £3.00 for 6hrs.** **See Donnie's advertisement opposite.**

HOWWOOD TROUT FISHERY - FLY ONLY - OPEN ALL YEAR

A natural loch of 8 acres with panoramic views of the surrounding rural countryside. This long established fishery enjoys a large number of natural insect hatches throughout the year and is as admirably suitable for the traditional fly fisher, wet, dry or nymphing as the rainbow lure angler. Situated just a mile above the village of Howwood on the A737 it's just a twenty minute drive from Glasgow. Stocked daily with full finned rainbow, brown, golden and brook trout there are fish in there from 11/2Lb. to 22lb. at least. The lodge is always warm and comfortable with snacks, tea and coffee always on the brew. Tackle wise apart from flies, lines and all the other wee bits there is a selection of rods to try before you buy. There is also qualified casting instruction available. **Day permits are £10.50 (9am - 4.30pm) with four fish then C & R; Any four hours is £8.0 with 2 fish then C & R; Father & Son day with 6 fish is £15.50.** **See the advertisement on opposite page**

LAWFIELD TROUT FISHERY - OPEN ALL YEAR
FLY ONLY AND BAIT POND

1999 is the tenth anniversary of this one of the longest established fisheries on the west coast of Scotland. The five acre loch is located in a valley just one mile above the lovely village of Kilmacolm. It is a peacefull and quiet setting where deer come to the loch to feed on the rushes. There are numerous hatches of natural fly throughout the season including Buzzers, Olives, Bloodworm, Sedge and Damsel's. The bait pond is a great fun attraction for families with kids. Picnic tables are provided, there's a heated fishing cabin with snacks avaiable and full toilet facilities. **Day ticket £14 (4 fish + C&R); £12 (3 fish + C&R); £8 Catch & Release; Parent & child (15) (7fish) £18; Junior (3 fish + C&R) £10; Half Day (2 fish + C&R) £8 Strictly 4Hrs. Call Billy on (01505) 874 182** **See adverisement on page 72**

DRUMMOND TROUT FARM AND FISHERY

Surely one of the best presented and successful fisheries in the country. Situated at Comrie, Perthshire just 10 miles from Loch Earn. The impulse angler will enjoy the rod rental facilities and the well stocked bait and beginners pools while the experienced fisher will find plenty of challenge at the specimen pool where fish to 16lb. 4ozs. have been caught. What a place for kids! Of all ages. Feed the fish or fish for your supper! See the salmon ladder at the riverside walkway. A great places for picnics or the farm shop and snacks are available.   **More details on opposite page.**

LOCH EARN FISHINGS

Loch Earn has a **Protection Order** in force. Anglers **must** purchase a permit before fishing. **Day permits for 1998 are £5.00; Junior £1; Weekly £12.00; Junior ££2.50** and are available at local shops and hotels. The loch has a great reputation for the high consistency of brown trout (native & stocked), char and occasional rainbow. Stocking is of 8000 3/4 to 21/2lb. brownies annually, so it is not surprising that fish of 3 to 5lb. are quite common. Spinning, bait and fly are permitted but not natural minnow. Boats for fishing or to take in the wonderful scenery and wildlife are available from **Drummond Estate Boats** at the **Drummond Fish Farm** just 11/2 miles east of Lochearnhead.   **More details on opposite page.**

73

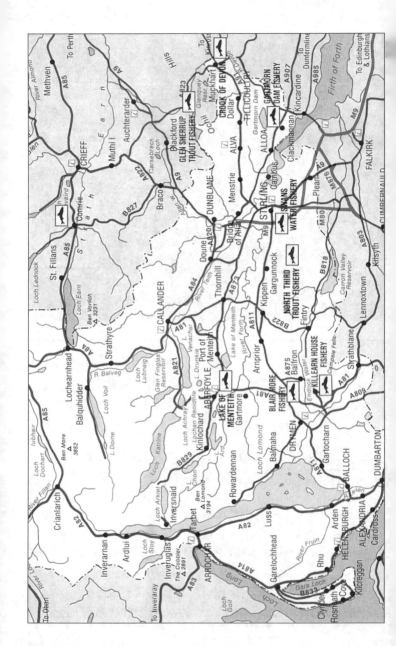

BUTTERSTONE LOCH - GATEWAY TO THE HIGHLANDS

Not a lot of miles to the north east of Stirling, Loch Earn and Glen Eagles is the village of Dunkeld on the A9 north of Perth. Situated as it is on the banks of the mighty River Tay this area is well used to welcoming the angler. Since 1974 a goodly number of these visitors come to fish the Butterstone Loch, only 3.5 miles from Dunkeld, for rainbow and to a lesser extent brown trout. The stocking of quality fresh fish twice a week provides a continued active fish population mainly of a perfect table size averaging 1lb 10oz. Location wise, it's the mature scenic majesty of the country side climbing towards the Highlands, the heather covered hills, the woodland and hill birds and diversity of colour that together make the day. The Fishing Lodge is spacious with modern toilets which include full disabled facilities. Fishing at Butterstone Loch is by FLY & BOAT ONLY. There are 19 boats, one of which is a wheely for use by disabled anglers. **Two sessions are available: 09:00 till 17:00 & 17:30 till Dusk. 1999 prices are: 1 man boat £16.00; 2 man boat £ 27:00; 3 man boat £32:00; Electric outboard hire £9.00. Catch limit 6 fish per angler.**

For further information and reservations refer below

PART 10

STIRLING - CARRON VALLEY - FALKIRK

There is a huge amount of fishing available within a few miles of Stirling. Salmon fishing on river and loch, Brown trout and rainbow on a great variety of natural Highland lochs with the addition of many top class fisheries.

This spectacular region can well provide both indoor and outdoor attractions for all ages and interests. Stirling with the Royal Castle, ancient buildings, and modern shopping and pedestrianised shopping streets are but a few minutes from the Highland splendour of the country and of course the River Forth on the very doorstep. For best tourist information visit the **Tourist Information Centre** on Dumbarton Road **Tel: (01786) 475 019** or on the M9/M80 motorway at Junction 9 **Tel: 01786) 814 111**. The only tackle shop in Stirling is **Mitchell's Tackle, 13 Bannockburn Road, St. Ninnians Tel: (01786) 445 587** is run by Mr. & Mrs. Mitchell who are very knowledgeable and experienced of all local waters. They have all the usual range of tackle plus some more, fly tying materials and local permits with certain parking right at the door. W. J. Scrimgeour. 28 New Market Street, Falkirk is run by Bill Campbell who dispenses a full range of tackle and local permits. Tron Sports at Tron Court in Tullibody has tackle and issues permits as does Country Pursuits in Bridge of Allan.

RIVER FORTH - STIRLING COUNCIL WATER

Salmon & Sea Trout   **Season: 1 Feb - 31 Oct.**

There are changes in regulation and rules for the 1999 season regarding the fishing for salmon on the Stirling Council stretch of the River Forth and the River Teith covered by issued season permits and concessionary permits. There are very clear instructions available from all permit issue points. The basis of the scheme is a tagging system which would appear to be quite straight forward and easy to implement. All season permit holders may legally keep a total of five salmon. Concessionary day permit holder may keep two salmon. Normal day permits and sea trout are not included in the scheme. Stirling Council make available day and season permits for salmon fishing on the Forth at Stirling and the Teith at Callander. We will deal only with the Stirling water here and the River Teith under the Callander section on page 86.

Generally, the Forth is slow, narrow and difficult to fish with spinner or fly and it is therefore from 1 May on when bait fishing commences that worming takes most salmon. Being for the most part close to the A84 and side roads, access is easy and convenient for parking. A very good map and regulation leaflet is issued with River Forth permits which for 1999 cost: **Resident day £12; Juvenile £6.00; Visitor (adult) £33; Juvenile £16.50; Over 60/Disabled £7.50;** Permits from: **Mitchell's Tackle, 13 Bannockburn Road** ; Country Pursuits, Bridge of Allan. **Various season tickets are also available. Information from: Stirling Council HQ, Tel: (01786) 442 936; Fax: (01786) 443 003; email: dixont@stirling.gov.uk**

SWANWATER FISHERY - OPEN ALL YEAR

With the reputation of being one of the better managed rainbow and brown trout fisheries the popular 7.5 acre Swanwater Lochan has 3 boats, easy access pathways and casting platforms around the banks. The Millpond is a 2 acre water with bank fishing only and Meadow Pond for beginners. Snacks are available and toilets (disabled access) in the reception area. Access is easy from the A872 at Bannockburn Heritage Centre and is well signposted. Rainbows averaged out at 1lb 14oz in 1997. Swanwater (1999) costs £18 for 8 hours (5 fish) Boat £6; £12 for 4 hours (3 fish) boat £4; £8 for 2 hours (2 fish) boat £3; The Millpond £14 - £9 - £6 and same limit. For bookings Tel: (01786) 814 805.

NORTH THIRD TROUT FISHERY - FLY ONLY

"Commended" by the Scottish Tourist Boards Visitor Attraction Scheme, 1998 was an all time record for this popular fishery with a total of 1,017 fish over 3lb. being recorded caught. This included 53 fish over 10lb. and 217 between 6 and 10lb. There is little doubt that the atrocious weather in late season as at most fisheries in Scotland reduced catches somewhat. With 23 boats and a 40 bank rods this rainbow and brown trout water is ideal for club outings and it is a very good idea to phone or book ahead, particularly at weekends. The 120 acre loch is hidden in the hill country four miles from Stirling and is expecting to be sing posted by the spring of 1999.

The season runs 15 March through 31 October and fishing is permitted from 10am daily. Natural fly on such a large and diverse loch allows well for both modern lure techniques and traditional methods. 10am - 5pm and 6pm - 11pm bank permits are £14 (10 fish); 10am - 11pm bank permits are £17 (no limit); Boats = 10am - 5pm 2 rods £28 (20 fish); 10am - 11pm 2 rods £37 (no limit). Bookings and info Tel: (01786) 471 967

LARBERT AND STENHOUSEMUIR ANGLING CLUB

Just a 15 minute drive from Stirling gets you to either of these club fishings which consist of Loch Coulter with good brown trout fishing and the River Carron with brown trout and at this stage occasional salmon and sea trout.

LOCH COULTER - Fly Only - Season: 1 April - 6 October

This popular brown trout loch is a reservoir controlled by the water board with the fishing administration by the club. No bank fishing is permitted but two of the boats are thoughtfully reserved for the casual visitor. Situated just north of Carron Bridge the situation is rural and peaceful in lovely scenery, no shortage of wild life belying central belt industry just out of site. Local flies are Grouse and Claret, Black Pennel, Greenwells and Blae and Black. Permits at £18 per day and boat keys are issued at **Topps Farm & Guest House. Fintry Road, Denny. Tel: (01324) 822 471** Which is just a mile east of the Carron Bridge Hotel on the B818.

RIVER CARRON - Season: 6 March - 6 October

This is a typical spate river which needs a good freshet to encourage salmon to run. Diligent clean up and thoughtful management and stocking over the last 10 years resulted in runs of salmon and silver trout slowly rebuilding in numbers. Sea trout are taken from early April and salmon from late April. Spinning, Worming and fly is permitted, but not prawn, shrimp or diving minnow. With the miles of river available access is varied from a walk of between 2 minutes and 2 miles. Sunday fishing for trout only is permitted with a restriction to 3lb B S nylon. Permits are a pittance at £4 per rod day with O A P's £2 and juniors £1 and can be purchased at: Paton, Newsagent, Larbert; McWatt Tackle, Main St, Carronshore; This & That, Stirling St, Denny; Topps Farm, and Scrimgeour Fishing Tackle, Falkirk. Local resident season tickets from: Larbert D I Y, Main St, Larbert Tel/Fax: (01324) 551 999 .

CARRON VALLEY RESERVOIR
SEASON: 19 April - 28 September   Fly only

This 965 acre water is headwater for both the River Endrick and the River Carron which flow in their respective directions from either end of the reservoir. No migratory fish however enter the reservoir. Lying as it is between the hills of Kilsyth and the Fintry Hills the Situation and outlook is rural and isolated surrounded by rather bleak moorland. The east end harbours the well maintained boats with the fishery office and car park adjacent. The eastern and south shores of the L shaped water are best favoured where many bays and headlands provide good trout lies as does the areas where the rivers Endrick and Carron outfall. Traditional Scottish loch flies are all that is required here, however, ensure you have a few 10s and even 8s for there is frequently a honkin' wind providing good waves with white caps. From Mid July on you should not be without Daddy Longlegs, Greenwells and big bushy Heather moths. **Boat fishing only, Weekdays £15 (2 rods) Weekends/evenings/holidays £20**. Advance bookings Tel: 01786 458 705; same day bookings Tel: 0374 832 525.

RIVER AVON
Excellent brown trout fishing is available on various stretches of this river which winds through most attractive countryside. Permits are most reasonable, access safe and easy, nice for family picnics and walking.
MUIRAVONSIDE COUNTRY PARK
Just 4 miles from Linlithgow on the B825 this lovely park has a 1 mile stretch of the river as a boundary. Any legal method is permitted with worm being the local favourite. Brownies are the main inhabitants. The average is 10 to 12ins with a few 1 to 2lbers taken each season. This is real peaceful fishing and surroundings, the whole family will enjoy it. Permits: £3.30 per rod day, juveniles £1.65 from the Park Visitor Centre Tel: (01506) 845 311.
AVON VALLEY ANGLING CLUB
Excellent value brown trout fishing season tickets available for this stocked section (Avonbridge Area) details from: Club Secretary. (01324) 862 276
SLAMANNAN ANGLING CLUB
This Slamannan area stretch can be fished by day ticket issued at Fit o' the Toon Bar, Slamannan for £3 per day juveniles £1.50.

UNION CANAL
Course fishing in the canal consists of pike, perch, roach, bream, tench, mirror and leather carp. Though fishing is free a permit is required from the Forth Valley Tourist Board, Falkirk Tel: (01506) 843 306.

GLEN DEVON TO BRIDGE OF ALLAN
From the Crook of Devon westward towards Callander there is without crossing the Forth a considerable amount of casual fishing available by day permits from: Tron Sports, Tullibody Tel: (01259) 215 499 and Country Pursuits, Bridge of Allan Tel: (01786) 834 495 issue permits and will point you in the right direction.

CROOK OF DEVON VILLAGE FISHERY
Just off the A977 in Crook of Devon village is this extensive multi pond fishery and fish farm. The ponds are designed in such a way you never feel there is a lot of area you cannot cast over. Parking is adjacent to the water with a cosy restaurant and shop to provide plenty of interest for the non fisher and tackle rental for the impulse fisher. Open from Easter to mid October this is a great place for those who want just to catch the breakfast, introduce the kids to catching trout or are serious fishing addicts. **It costs you just £4 to fish (Fly only) as long as you care and you pay just £2.00 per pound for the fish you catch.**
See advertisement page 82

ORCHILL TROUT FISHERY - FLY ONLY - OPEN ALL YEAR
Hundreds of natural wild brown trout inhabit this old estate loch which is set in a mature treed glade and fed by both burn and spring so ensuring that even in the heat of summer the fish are kept fresh and active. Elizabeth Jackson the owner ensures daily stockings of 1.5lb. to 7lb. hard fighting rainbows of good quality. The loch is of very easy access the car park being adjacent to the Chalet where free tea and coffee are always available. The loch is of 4.5 acres and is mainly fished from the banking although there are two boats available. The loch is located just off the Gleneagles/Braco Road which is off the A822 or the A823. This is an A S S F water. **Session permits: 4 hours £12 (3 fish); Day £20.00 (5 fish) Evening £12.00 (3fish)** For brochure, reservations or more information call Elizabeth on **Tel: (01764) 682 287**
See advertisement page 82

DEVON ANGLING ASSOCIATION

Founded in 1905 by a group of local "gentlemen" it would be fair to say the association has flourished for it now controls fishing on 11 miles of both banks of the River Devon and Glenquey reservoir. Both the river and reservoir are stocked with bank and other improvements an ongoing program. Day permits are available locally, season tickets only by post from the secretary: R. Breingan Esq,. 33 Redwell Pl, Alloa Tel: 01259 215 185.

RIVER DEVON

SEASON: **BROWN TROUT 15 MARCH - 6 OCT.**

                  SALMON & SEA TROUT 15 MARCH - 31 OCT.

The river is **FLY ONLY** for the first month of the season and thereafter is open to any legal method and it is the worm I am told that takes the majority of salmon. The water flow on the river is determined by the outflow from Castlehill reservoir and is of a minimum of 6,000,000 gallons a day which is fine for fishing but quickly becomes coloured if run off occurs with heavy rain. Brownies of 9 to 11ins are in going stock annually so there must be quite a good head of specimens not to mention the rainbow escapees which are now becoming almost commonplace in many rivers. Grilse of 5 to 10 lb are the norm with a few heavier salmon. Access is mostly easy thanks to the map issued with permits. And there are plenty of good places for a picnic. Day permits are £4 for brown trout and £15 for salmon & sea trout and are issued from 14 outlets including Country Pursuits, Crockharts, Scrimgeours.

GLENQUEY RESERVOIR   **SEASON 1 APRIL - 30 SEP.**

Situated about a mile off the A823 north of Yetts of Muckart the road end is adjacent to the entrance to Castlehill reservoir. A good car park is about a 1/2 mile from the water. There are no boats on this fly only water but plenty of banking which is easy to walk. Stocked as it is annually with 9 to 11 inch trout the returns are excellent. Typical Scottish flies size 14 & 16 do well with the locals in favour of Blae & Black, Soldier Palmer, Invicta and the Butchers. A light warm westerly is the favoured breeze. April and May do well, perhaps due in part to the autumn stocking. 5 adult and 2 junior permits are available daily at £7 and are issued from Muckhart Post Office.

ALLAN WATER ANGLING IMPROVEMENT ASSOCIATION

The association controls the majority of the fishing on Allan Water. Though the source is to the north of Blackford it is however well below the Braco road bridge before there is other than semblance of fishable pools. From Kimbuck down passed the Ashfield dam and on through Dunblain to Kippenross the fishing improves though there are rapids downstream then under the footbridge to some of the most popular pools on the river. From the weirs at Bridge of Allan to the junction with the Forth flat fields dictate a meandering progress. There is plenty of easy access to the river and many places where family or non fishers can picnic, always of course taking their trash with them on departure. There are three beats with 5 rods permitted on each. Day tickets to fish for brown trout, salmon and sea trout, (Monday - Friday only) are £5 per rod until 1 July then £15 thereafter; Season tickets for locals are £35, juniors and O A P £12; Visitors £40, juniors and O A P £15. Permits from Country Pursuits, Bridge of Allan Tel: (01786) 834 495

GARTMORN DAM FISHERY
BROWN & RAINBOW TROUT   SEASON: 1 APRIL - 4 OCTOBER

Situated in the Gartmorn Dam Country Parks 215 acres this loch has justly a reputation for top quality brown trout fishing. This will be supplemented in 1999 with introduction of 8000 X 3/4 to 1lb. and a good number of 4 to 6lb rainbow trout. The water is 167 acres with ample room for the 11 boats (fly only) one of which is a wheely. Spinning is restricted to specific bank sections.

The location is picturesque with great views over the Ochill Hills and is probably the most scenic parkland in the central belt.

Though lures do well early in the season (Ace of Spades, Viva, Muddler Minnow) in cool water as the season progresses the Scottish traditional fly patterns are top: Grouse & Claret, Black Pennell, Soldier Palmer, the writers own favourite is Dark Mackerel.

Sessions are 09:00 till 17:00 & 17:00 till Dusk; Bank permits: £6.20; Concession £4.90; Junior £1.70; Boats, 2 rods £22.80, I rod £11.00; Concession £13.50; Season permits are also available. Further information & bookings out of season **Tel: (01259) 213131.** In season the **Gartmorn Country Park Visitor Centre Tel: (01259) 214 319.**

PART ELEVEN
CALLANDER - ABERFOYLE - TROSSACHS

With a choice of river and loch fishing for brown trout, salmon and sea trout that could keep you going all season. Choice could be a problem! However, just wander along to **JAMES BAYNE FISHING TACKLE** at 72 Main Street, Callander and Dougie Allan who is tops with local experience and knowledge, has permits for a list of waters the length of your arm and all the tackle you will ever need.

For non fishers or for a wee change there is no shortage of attractions after you call at the **TOURIST INFORMATION CENTRE Tel: (01786) 824 428** where you will get best assistance with your inquiries and have the opportunity to spend some time in the **Rob Roy & Trossachs Visitor Centre**. There are delightfully attractive walks right off the Main Street. The Falls of Leny, the Trossachs Trail, Queen Elizabeth Forestry Park with a visitor centre near Aberfoyle or a cruise on the spectacular Loch Katrine are all very accessible.

RIVER TEITH

Fed from the lochs Katrine, Venachar, Achray and Finglas Reservoir to the south west and lochs Doine, Voil and Lubnaig to the north together with mountain side run off the Teith is fortunate that the northern loch group is relatively free running and not harnessed as water supply as with the first group to Glasgow and the central belt.

STIRLING COUNCIL WATER - CALLANDER

SEASON:	SALMON & SEA TROUT	1 FEB - 31 OCT
	BROWN TROUT	15 MARCH - 6 OCT

There are changes in regulation and rules for the 1999 season regarding the fishing for salmon on the Stirling Council stretch of the River Forth and the River Teith covered by issued season permits and concessionary permits. Very clear instructions are available from all permit issue points.

The river takes some shape and character at Callander and it is here that the Town Water is available by day and season permit to both local and visitor. This town beat has 7 good pools and other good fishing water which is much dependant on wet weather to create a freshet. The top 4 pools are separated from the others by the **Roman Camp Country House Hotel private stretch,** this however entails only a short walk to bypass. Salmon in excess of 20lb are taken from this water each season as are some fine sea trout. There is an excellent map supplied with permits which also highlights regulations and lists other council waters. Bait fishing is not permitted until 1 April after which date only prawn/shrimp are prohibited. This is a well managed water which bailiffs patrol. Permits for the Teith are issued by **James Bayne Fishing Tackle** in Callander; **Mitchell's Tackle**, Stirling and Country Pursuits, Bridge of Allan : **Resident adult £10 per day, £36 season; Juvenile £5, £18 season; Visitor £25 per day, £105 season; Visitor juvenile £12.50, season £52.**

GART FARM FISHINGS
The Gart fishings are situated some 2 miles downstream of Callander comprising of about 1 mile single north bank with 2 rods permitted daily the owner reserving the rights of 2 additional rods for occasional use. A season rod for this stretch is £234.00 plus VAT. Day permits are £30 Feb - April; £20 May - July; £40 August - September; £50 October.

CAMBUSMORE FISHINGS
With 26 named pools providing beautiful runs, streams and glides this single and double bank stretch is quality fly water, though spinning is permitted. There are three beats each of which can facilitate up to 3 rods. Spring fishing can produce exciting rewards here, though September and October are the prime months with the last three year average 138 salmon. Sole agent: Country Pursuits Tel: (01786) 834 495

RIVER LENY - SALMON - SEA TROUT - 1 FEB - 30 OCT
A mile long stretch from Loch Lubnaig down has 5 daily rods available at only £15.00 each. Spinning and fly are permitted, it great in October/September so book early. Cameron Tel: (01232) 246 525.

ABERFOYLE - STRATHARD - TROSSACHS
This peaceful holiday village provides the requirements of visitors from all corners of the world. Surrounded as it is by glens and straths with rivers and lochs of outstanding scenic grandeur with a mist of history and ancient culture ever present. There is fishing aplenty here, names which are readily dropped in conversations anywhere anglers meet. Loch

Ard and **Trossachs' Fishings** are enterprising angling locations at **Loch Finglas**, **Loch Arklet, Loch Katrine, Loch Venachar** and Lake of Menteith the list goes on and on. With the initiative of Forest Enterprise more waters are being made available with easy access, safe traverse and picnic sites. A early call in planning should be to the **Tourist Information Centre Tel: (01877) 382 352** Main Street, Aberfoyle where details of interest and entertainment features are available. The **Rob Roy Motel** as you enter the Village is a popular modern facility serving casual bar meals. Just walking distance from Loch Ard for which they issue permits the **Inverard Hotel** on the B829 is an experienced fishers Hostelry set overlooking the River Forth. The Altskeith Hotel is also on the B829 set in mature surroundings overlooking lovely Loch Ard.

FISHING IN ABERFOYLE FOREST DISTRICT

Best plan is to visit the **Forest Park Visitor Centre Tel: (01877) 382 258** in Aberfoyle (open Easter - October) Permits for the River Forth are only issued by Addison's Newsagent, Aberfoyle and for the lochs at: **Bayne Fishing Tackle,** Callander, and **MacFarlane's Boatyard**, Balmaha. There is a £1.50 day concession permit for under 16's for Trout, Pike and Perch only.

RIVER FORTH - by ABERFOYLE
Salmon: 1 Feb - 31 October £5.50 per day - No Sunday fishing
Sea Trout 1 Feb - 15 October £5.50 per day - No Sunday fishing
Brown Trout: 15 March - 6 October £3 per day - No Sunday fishing

LOCH CHON
Pike & Perch: All year £3 per day - Bank fishing only
Brown Trout: 15 March - 6 October £3 per day - Bank fishing only

LOCH DRUNKIE
Brown Trout: 15 March - 6 October £3 per day - Bank fishing only, access via Forest Drive for vehicles, from car park on foot.

LOCH REOIDHTE
Brown Trout: 15 March - 6 October £5 per day - Fly only from bank. Access as Drunkie. Permits only from Visitor Centre.

LOCH LUBNAIG
Salmon: 1 Feb - 31 October £5.50 per day - No Sunday fishing
Sea Trout: 1 Feb - 31 October £5.50 per day - No Sunday fishing
Brown Trout: 15 March - 6 October £3 per day

The Inverard is a family run hotel set amidst spectacular scenery in the heart of the Trossachs, Aberfoyle.

Loch Ard fly fishing permits provided **free of charge** to all hotel guests.

Overlooking the River Forth, within easy walking distance of **Loch Ard** you are only minutes away from a day's **fly fishing** (instruction can be arranged). 10 mins by car from the **Lake of Menteith** (fly only) and **Lochs Chon, Drunkie** and **Achray** where **bait and spinning** are permitted.

Lochard Road, Aberfoyle,
The trossachs FK8 3TD
Phone: 01877 382229
* 25 mins from Stirling
* 45 mins to Glasgow
* 1 hour to Edinburgh

* Award Winning Restaurant
* Traditional Scottish menu
* Plus, Scotland's only Filipino Restaurant

We are an ideal base from which to see Scotland
2 mins drive from 18 hole golf course, cycle paths & walks abound.

THE ROB ROY MOTEL
Aberfoyle - Stirlingshire - FK8 3UX
Tel: (01877) 382 245 Fax: (01877) 382 262

Situated at the gateway to the Trossachs the ROB ROY is local to such great fishing as the Lake of Menteith, Loch Katrine, Loch Arklet, Loch Achray and Loch Drunkie. There is an 18-hole golf course opposite the Motel, forest walks, horse riding, windsurfing and mountain bikes available locally.

- SPECIAL RATES FOR ANGLERS
- EARLY BREAKFAST
- HOT MEALS TILL 10 PM
- PACKED LUNCHES
- FREEZER FACILITIES
- ALL ROOMS EN SUITE + COLOUR TV
- WEEKEND SPECIALS OCTOBER THROUGH APRIL

LAKE OF MENTEITH - FLY FISHING ONLY
RAINBOW & BROWN TROUT - Season: 4 April - 31 Oct 1998

One of Scotland's best known beauty spots The Lake of Menteith is stocked with up to 1000 1 to 5lb rainbow every week of the main season with the addition of 1 to 2lb brownies intermittently. Situated off the B8034 off the A81 Glasgow to Callander road at Aberfoyle. Parking, toilet facilities and a hut adjacent to the boat launch area.

The generous limits are realistic and frequently achieved. A day here is also a wildlife experience. Designated a Site of Scientific Interest that supreme angler the Osprey is frequently seen to treat catch limits with some degree of contempt! A boat only water, traditional flies and methods with Dunkeld, Zulu, Soldier Palmer, and Worm Fly are as rewarding as are lure techniques.

James Kyle operates his **School of Fly Fishing** here where a unique learning experience and exceptional fishing is assured. Enquiries **Tel: (01416) 399 631**

Charges on boats are for two rods. Day session: Mon/Fri 9.30 - 5.30 £27; Sat £30 per boat (18 fish); Evening Session: 28 April - 26 July 6pm - 11pm Mon/Thur £21 Fri/Sat £24 (18 fish); Evening session: 28 July - 23 Aug 6pm - 9.30pm £12 (12 fish); Sunday Session: 12 noon - 7pm £30 (18 fish). Tel: (01877) 385 664

LOCH ARD

Situated close to the B829 on the outskirts of Aberfoyle this lovely loch is fly only and can be bank or boat fished for wild brown trout. Stocked intermittently, access is easy and just a stroll from the village. Day permits are £2.50, season £25, 50% reduction for OAP's are issued from the Farm Shop at Kinlochard who also handles the Boat rental at £10 per day, Altskeith Hotel who also has boats and **Inverard Hotel** by the road side over looking the River Forth on the way to the loch.

TROSSACH'S FISHINGS 15 MARCH - 6 OCTOBER

With such a great selection of excellent fishing lochs **Trossach's Fishings** must be a good bet to arrange consecutive days of fishing with confidence.

Boats are £20.00 per session, 3 rods fishing. Outboards (Venachar only) £7.00. Katrine, Arklet, Finglas are FLY ONLY & bank fishing while **Loch Achray is FLY ONLY from boats no bank fishing. Sessions: 09.30 - 17.30 & 18.00 - 23.00. No catch limit.**

Permits for all lochs are available in the cabin at Loch Venachar on the north shore of the loch on the A821 one mile east of Brig O'Turk.

For information or bookings **Tel: (01786) 841 692. Mbl: 0850 558869**

LOCH VENACHAR - Brown Trout - Sea Trout - Course fish

This loch fishes well from opening day on 15 March when Grouse and Claret, Black Pennel, Ke He and Black and Peacock Spider are a good choice. Spinning, bait, trolling and fly permitted.

Bank fishing permits are available at £6.00 per day , £4.00 for under 16's from **James Bayne, Fishing Tackle, Main Street. Callander.**

LOCH KATRINE - Brown Trout - Fly & boat only

At the west end of the A821 from Callander or Aberfoyle this loch set in wonderful Highland surrounding you will not want to leave after a day in affray with the wild broon troot which inhabit this big loch. All the usual Highland dark flies will do great here until mid July when big hairy Heather Moths, wet or dry bring the big fellows crashing through the waves.

LOCH ARKLET - Brown Trout - Fly & Boat only

About 12 miles west of Aberfoyle on the B829 this is a wee bit smaller than Katrine and lies west to east which gives a better wave when the wind is from the west and to a lesser extent from the east. Magic scenery in peace and quiet prevail here. No catch limit here for 1998.

GLEN FINGLAS RESERVOIR - Brown Trout - Boat only

Situated just a mile off the A821 at Brig O' Turk the access road leads to the south end of this deep loch. Brown trout are in good condition from late March and are mostly taken while drifting the shallow shoulders fishing traditional Highland fur and feather. No catch limit here for 1998.

LOCH ACHRAY - Brown Trout - Fly & boat only

Great traditional boat wild brown trout fishing on this loch with 8 boats

available. Flies and conditions as above. **See advertisement page 90**
LOCHS LUBNAIG - VOIL - EARN - TAY - RIVER BALVAG
LOCH LUBNAIG - Brown Trout - Perch

With access directly off the A84 just north of Callander, plenty of easy parking and picnic areas make this a popular place in the summer. Permits are just £4 per day or £10 a week with kids at half price. All legal methods are permitted. Permits: **James Bayne Fishing Tackle**
LOCH VOIL - Salmon - Brown Trout

Take the Balquidder road off the A84 at the Kingshouse Hotel to reach the north shore of the easy access loch where there are plenty of great picnic spots for the kids or non fishers. Bank fishing is just £3.00 per day and kids £1.50. Permits from: Calum Marshall, Crigrui, Balquidder or **James Bayne Fishing Tackle**
RIVER BALVAG - SALMON

A two mile stretch of this wee highland stream is available for spinning, fly or bait fishing. If you are lucky enough to be there when there is a bit of rain run off you could be frying tonight with fresh salmon on the menu. Permits £3.00 from: **James Bayne Fishing Tackle.**

LOCH EARN - Brown Trout - Rainbow - Char
 Day permits are £5.00, Weekly £12.00, Juniors £1 and Weekly £2.50 and are available at most post offices, hotels and caravan parks around the loch side. **Drummond Estate Boats come with 4HP motor, fuel and life jackets. 4 hours £15; 6 hours £22; 8 hours £29.**
Turn right off the A84 on to the A85 at Lochearnhead. This road hugs the north shore most of way along the 61/2 mile length of the loch. Just a mile and a bit along is **Drummond Estates Boat Hire** is located at the **Drummond Fish Farm**.
The loch fishing is managed by **Loch Earn Fishings** who have stocked for seven years now with 8000 brownies from 11/2 to 21/2lb. So don't come the "there's nae' fish in't" if your such a dumplin' as to blank here. The 1998 season saw a continuing increase in permit sales which reflects the growing reputation of the loch which is now well established as one of Scotlands premier brown trout waters. Returns substantiate this with the 857 brownies an average of 1.25lb, 350 rainbows averaged just shy of 1.50lb. and 99 char over the 1lb. mark. The heaviest brown was 9lb 14oz taken by Rab Macdonald of Larbert. Best rainbow

was 10lb 7oz. by 13 year old Hayley Beckinsdale from Wigan. John McCarther from Larbert took the heaviest char at 5lb 14oz.

Spinning and trolling favoured hardware are **Scottish made Bridun** Rotobate spoons, Flickerbait, Flutter spoons and **ABU** Dropfish, Drop-pen and the old favourite Toby a sure attractor. Scottish flies to ensure aggressive reaction are Coachman, Black Pennell, Kate McLaren, Invicta, Yellow Gosling, Daddy Longlegs, Olive & Claret Hoppers while the writers own choice would be Invicta on the top, Greenwells in the middle and Dark Mackerel at the tip all size 14. However, if there is a decent wave, up to size 10 with a Muddler Minnow on the bob.

For Information & booking: Drummond Estates Boat Hire or Drummond Trout Farm and Fishery See Page 73.

For Loch Earn Fishings Tel: (01764) 681 257. Fax: (01764)681 550

KILLIN - LOCH TAY - RIVER DOCHART

The tidy wee village of Killin sits on the banks of the River Dochart at the west end of loch Tay where huge salmon and brownies are landed each season. Jack Rough Fishing Tackle Tel: (01567) 820 362 is on the Main Street and issues permits.

KILLIN BREADALBANE ANGLING CLUB

The club permit allows fishing for trout and Pike on a stretch of the River Dochart, the River Lochay and some banking on the shores of Loch Tay. An excellent map is issued on the permit and at only £4 per day or £12.50 a week is top value. The rivers are of course Highland spate rivers which require rain to provide productive results. Permits from: J H Rough & J R News

AUCHLYNE - SUIE - BOVAIN ESTATE FISHING

Some fishing is generally available on this stretch of the River Dochart by permit from the Glendochart Caravan Park. The charge is for 98' £4 per day for trout; £6 per day for Salmon. Any legal method is permitted.

LOCH TAY - Salmon - Trout - Course fish

Situated on the northern Loch shore Loch Tay lodges and cottages are great for family holidays. Salmon fishing. Short breaks are available from 15 January through May. Weekday Salmon fishing at £35 includes boat, engine, fuel and permit, Saturday is £40; Trout fishing is £25 per day. More information or bookings Tel: (01567) 820 323 Fax: 820 581.

MORTON FISHERY

Mid Calder, West Lothian

Open 27 Feb - 30 Oct 1999

A well established Fishery of 22 acres which is proving to be increasingly popular with Anglers. We place great emphasis on the quality of the Rainbow Trout which are stocked at least twice weekly throughout the Season.
10 boats are available for all
Sessions plus good Bank Fishing.

Bookings and further information:
Tel: 01506 882293

TROUTMASTER WATER

OPEN ALL YEAR

ALLANDALE TARN FISHERIES

WEST CALDER, WEST LOTHIAN   TELEPHONE/FAX: (01506) 873073

★ One of the leading small trout waters in Scotland
★ Superb dry fly and nymph fishing   ★ Fly only loch
1½ - 18lb   ★ Rainbow, brown, golden & blue trout
★ Iona bait pool - rainbow & brown, golden &tiger
trout   ★ Quality fish stocked daily - 1½lb to 18lb
★ Heavybasket competition last Saturday every
month   ★ Rod hire & tackle sales & tuition available

WEST LOTHIAN FISHERIES OF DISTINCTION

Just a short drive from Edinburgh and a little more from Glasgow there are two fisheries which should not be missed. Both are set in mature country locations which belie there proximity to urbanism. Both are **A S S F member fisheries** so provide a warm welcome and quality sport.

MORTON FISHERY - FLY ONLY - OPEN 27 FEB - 30 OCT

This well established fishery has a strong following of returning regulars! now that's reputation. Quality of fish has always been a hall mark of MORTON with stockings at least twice a week throughout the season. The 22 acres has 10 boats which is a very fair concentration with no crowding problems. Bank fishing is efficient with easy traverse though it should be noted that it is boat fishing only Thursday, Friday and Saturday. There are various prizes up for grabs such as heaviest fish of the week and best basket of the month. Evening sessions from 5.30 till dusk are held from May through August. and all night sessions are from 29 May through 1 August. **Bank fishing is £14.50 with 5 fish from 9.30am till 5pm; £12.00 with 4 fish 5.30 till dusk; Any 4 hrs with 3 fish is £10.00; Boats are £4.00 per session additional.** There are various C & R on limits available. **Julie Hewat** the owner is SANA qualified and offers casting instruction.   **See Julies advertisement on page 95**

ALLANDALE TARN FISHERIES - OPEN ALL YEAR

"One of the leading small trout waters in Scotland" is a quote that regulars here certainly agree with. A warm welcome is always extended both to individuals and club groups. The Fishing Lodge serves snacks, has rods for hire and a selection of tackle. Well designed and functional casting platforms round the perimeter of the loch make for comfortable casting in even the wildest condition. Margo Allan who manages the fishery looks on the high intensity of natural flying and terestrial insects from the mature tree surounds as a real bonus to fly fishers who prefer dry fly and nymph fishing. Stocking is a daily occurance with rainbow, blues, golden and brown trout from 1.5lb to 18lb. in residance. New for 1999 is the Iona Bait Pool also stocked daily. Casting insrtuction and coaching is on hand by Paul Buchan the Scottish Internationalist. Current charges are: **Iona Bait Pool. Full day £14.00 (4 fish); 4 Hours £9.00(2 fish); Allandale Tarn. All C & R after limit.Full day £15.00 (5 fish); 4 Hours £10.0 (3 fish); Evening Session £13.00 (4 fish).**

See advertisement page 95